Sweeter

than

Honey

*"How sweet are thy words unto my taste!
Yea, sweeter than honey to my mouth."
(Psalm 119:103)*

Joie & Audrey, I pray that God's Word will always be Sweeter than Honey to you. In His love, Jane Ps. 119:103

Sweeter than Honey

A guide to effective Bible study

and the background of

how we got our Bible

Jesse B. Deloe Jan. 18, 1990

Jesse B. Deloe

BMH Books

Winona Lake, Indiana 46590

Dedication

To Gladys, whose companionship in life
and the Lord is another of God's wonderful gifts

Cover design by Tim Kennedy

ISBN: 0-88469-105-5

COPYRIGHT 1979
BMH BOOKS
WINONA LAKE, INDIANA

Printed in U.S.A.

Preface

"The Bible, the whole Bible, and nothing but the Bible." That's the long-standing motto of the Brethren Church. Why, then, don't we just study the Bible and forget books about the Bible? The reader must keep in mind that the volume he holds in his hands now is one in a series of *Bible study guides.* The books in this series are intended to guide the student into and through the Bible. The Bible remains the textbook. At best, these guides are study aids. This particular guide is not a Bible study but a study about the Bible. Hopefully, it will aid the reader better to undertake the investigation of the Bible in subsequent studies.

The writer has constantly had in his mind the ultimate audience for this guide—the Sunday School class. In particular, he has written it with the Koinonia Class of the Winona Lake Brethren Sunday School in mind. He has continually asked himself, "Now, how will I teach this chapter—or make this point—to the Koinonia Class?" He has taught that class for more than three years and considers it one of the great joys of his ministry. If those class members profit from this volume, as he endeavors to lead them in a study about the Bible, his effort will be sufficiently rewarded.

Indebted to his own teachers—Sunday School, college, seminary, and others whose lectures, seminars, books, and magazine articles have been helpful to him—the writer acknowledges that this is largely their work.

Study the Bible to be wise;
Believe it to be safe;
Practice it to be holy.

Jesse B. Deloe   Winona Lake, Indiana
                                            January, 1979

Introduction

The Bible has been called "the light that will not go out." It has been described as the anvil upon which multitudes of hammers have been worn out, but which yet remains unchanged and unmarked by their blows. Samuel Chadwick describes it this way:

> I have guided my life by the Bible for more than 60 years, and I tell you there is no book like it. It is a miracle of literature, a perennial spring of wisdom, a wonder of surprises, a revelation of mystery, an infallible guide of conduct, and an unspeakable source of comfort. Pay no attention to people who discredit it, for I tell you that they speak without knowledge. It is the Word of God itself. Study it according to its own direction. Live by its principles, believe its message, and follow its precepts. No man is uneducated who knows the Bible, and no one is wise who is ignorant of its teachings! (*Our Daily Bread*)

It is one of the marvels of the book, however, that it is capable of understanding by a child. Richard Placeway, in a *Daily Devotions* article some years ago, referred to Robert Gunning's study that placed certain publications according to the simplicity of their reader's understanding. In his "Fog Index" he noted that *Time* magazine requires 10 years of schooling; *Reader's Digest* requires only 8 years, but the Bible, for the most part, demands but 6 or 7 years. "Suffer the little children to come unto me," Jesus said. (Mark 10:14) And they can, with understanding from the Bible!

Bibles come in all forms and sizes. They are available in book bindings, loose-leaf notebooks, magazine style, records, tapes. The writer has in his possession the entire King James Version Bible (1,245 pages) on a 1-inch square piece of microfilm. On the small slide, 773,746 words are miniaturized—

and it takes a special magnifying viewer to read it. But it's all there!

No other book in history has been preserved in such a variety of forms, for such a long period of time, against such opposition. To some, it is considered a dangerous book. The story is told of a Soviet official who was asked why a study of the Bible was frowned upon in his country and why those who dared to print and distribute it were severely punished. He replied, "We find that the reading of this book changes people in a way that is dangerous to our state!" Indeed, if we will be faithful to study God's Word and allow His Spirit to work the Word in our lives, we will be changed!

In this small volume, it will be our purpose to examine some of the basic considerations of the Bible—its origin, arrangement, marvels, reliability, and use—and many others.

Table of Contents

1

The Importance
of the Bible

I. **The Bible Is the Self-Revelation of God**
    A. We could not know God without the Bible
    B. We would not know Jesus without the Bible

II. **The Bible Is our Supreme Authority**
    A. Why it is authoritative
    B. How it is authoritative

III. **The Bible Is Sufficient for the Christian**
    A. The purpose of the Bible
    B. The scope of the Bible

This chapter may appear to the average reader of this study guide to be unnecessary. If he did not consider the Bible to be important, he very likely would not be opening the covers of this brief volume. However, a review of the values of "the Book of books" may prove to be helpful. We regard the Bible to be important because it reveals God; in fact, it is His revelation of Himself. In that sense it is, indeed, the Word of God. The Bible is important, also, because it is authoritative, the supreme authority to the Church and the Christian—again, because it is the Word of God. Furthermore, the Bible is sufficient for the needs of modern man. That reason alone, of course, would make it important to us.

I. The Bible Is the Self-Revelation of God

The Scriptures tell us that God can be known—or at least some things about God can be known—through many avenues. We can learn of Him from nature. "The heavens declare the glory of God; and the firmament sheweth his handywork" (Ps. 19:1). Since man is made in the image of God, something about the Creator can be learned by knowing the creature—even though it is a marred image because of man's fall into sin. Conscience may be another avenue to discern something about right and wrong, thus gaining some small idea of the nature of God. But, all of these are incomplete.

A. We could not know God without the Bible. The opening words of the Bible, "In the beginning God . . . ." (Gen. 1:1), introduce one who is not only omnipotent—as the creation demonstrates—but one for whom there can be no definitive introduction. From the day of that beginning, men have dreamed up their gods; they have sensed a void in their hearts without a supreme being, so they have created one in their image and to their liking. But, that is not the God of the Bible. What we know about God is not the subjective imaginings or reasonings of our minds; it is the absolute revelation of His Word. We can say what God is like because He has chosen to tell us what He's like.

Without the Bible we may see something of what God has

done—again, creation is a prime example—but we cannot identify who did it or what His purposes were in doing it. The Bible answers these questions. The so-called "general" or "natural revelation" of God is available to all who study nature, but the Bible is a very special revelation. Only to the seeker of truth as given in this special revelation can God be known in a personal, specific way. A knowledge of God through general revelation might result in awe or even worship, but one must personally respond to the special revelation of God as redeemer in order to become an accepted part of the family of God.

This self-revelation of God was not an all-at-once declaration of fact. No, God worked over centuries and through various means to reveal Himself. He fellowshipped with some (Adam in the Garden of Eden), spoke to others (Moses at the burning bush), revealed hidden things in dreams (Daniel, Joseph). Through the thundering prophets of the Old Testament, He made known His holiness and His righteous demands. From the pens of the apostles He revealed His plan and purpose. And so it is that God's revelation of Himself has been progressive. Is it complete yet? Is there more we might expect?

The Scriptures have the answers to these questions, too. "God, who at sundry [different] times and in divers [various] manners spake in time past unto the fathers by the prophets, Hath in these last days spoken unto us by his Son, whom he hath appointed heir of all things . . . ." (Heb. 1:1-2). Jesus Christ is the final revelation of God to men. He is "the brightness of his glory, and the express image of his person," (Heb. 1:3). Jesus is "the image of the invisible God . . . . " and "in him dwelleth all the fulness of the Godhead bodily" (Col. 1: 15, 2:9). Jesus testified that He was the expression of the Father. He said to Philip, who wanted to see the Father: "Have I been so long time with you, and yet hast thou not known me, Philip? he that hath seen me hath seen the Father . . . . " (John 14:9).

B. We would not know Jesus without the Bible. Men can know of God without knowing the Bible. Paul writes in the first chapter of his Epistle to the Romans that knowledge of God can be gained from the creation. But, it's the Bible that reveals the personal and sovereign God; and it's the Bible that reveals Jesus Christ as the clearest expression of God to men. And what do we know about Jesus? The Bible is the primary source of the information we have about God's son.

Secular history—and certainly early religious and church history—tell about the Jewish teacher, Jesus of Nazareth. But even the historical facts of His life are to be found most fully in the New Testament. As far as the significance of His coming, His life, death, and resurrection—only the Bible reveals these important matters. The Old Testament anticipates His coming; parts of it even prefigure the Messiah. The Gospels record the events of His life and death. The Book of Acts demonstrates His power as evidenced in His followers; the Epistles explain His ministry and what is yet to be completed; and the Revelation carries the story of Jesus into a time beyond time—the culmination of history. (See chapters 11 and 12.)

An All-American football player at the University of Colorado in the early '60s was an outstanding scholar and a Christian. When asked to share his testimony, he wrote that his interest in science as a youth led him to the belief that there must be a God. He was satisfied that only God could have brought into existence and sustained what he saw in his telescope and microscope. He went on to say, however, that science did not reveal to him who this God was. It was only through a study of the Bible that he came to know God through His Son, Jesus Christ.

Joe Romig, All-American offensive lineman, was exactly right. The world may recognize a God, but it can never find God or know Him personally by its searchings and reasonings. Had God not chosen to reveal Himself, mankind could not have discovered Him. Praise God, He has revealed Himself!

Study the Bible, and you'll come to know Him whom you could not otherwise find.

II. The Bible Is Our Supreme Authority

The question of authority is always a relevant question. Why should I submit to anyone's authority? Why should I obey? What makes another person more authoritative than I? Why should I accept an ancient book as final authority over my life? It is not only of an ancient society that these words could truthfully be recorded: "Every man did that which was right in his own eyes" (Judges 17:6, 21:25). The same could be written about any age—and for the same reason: "In those days there was no king in Israel" (same verses). When there is no acknowledgment of higher authority, men regard themselves as their own authority.

The Bible does not attempt to prove its right to demand obedience and submission. No lengthy treatises are written in its chapters to show that the Scriptures are authority, but its demands are implicit in its content. There is an abundance of evidence accompanying its precepts that demonstrates that the man who obeys is blessed of God (read the Psalms and Proverbs for examples).

The question of authority is not merely a twentieth century problem. It began in Genesis when the serpent asked Eve, "Hath God said" (Gen. 3:1). He was not arguing that God hadn't spoken—that was an indisputable fact. But he was implying that God's word was not to be taken as final; it was not to be accepted as authoritative. Doubt was cast in Eve's mind. So it has been, then, from the very beginning.

A. Why it is authoritative. Let us list some reasons for accepting the authority of the Bible. The following arguments have been offered by John R. Stott:

1. The historic Christian churches have consistently maintained and defended the divine origin of Scripture.
2. The Biblical writers themselves claimed authority.
3. The book's remarkable unity and cohesiveness, its ful-

filled prophecy, its nobility and dignity, its relevance.

4. Its power and influence.

5. What Jesus said about it.

(John R. Stott: "Jesus Christ and the Authority of the Word of God," *World Vision,* April 1974)

Lewis Sperry Chafer is quoted as giving similar arguments:

1. The Scriptures are authoritative, being God-breathed.

2. . . . being written by chosen men who were "borne along" by the Holy Spirit.

3. . . . being accredited by those who first received them.

4. . . . being attested by the Lord Jesus Christ, the second person of the Godhead.

5. . . . being received, delivered, and attested by the prophets (and, we might add, the apostles).

6. . . . being the Word employed by God the Holy Spirit.

7. The authority of the Bible is seen in the fact that without the slightest deflection it vindicates and satisfies its every claim.

(Quoted by Roger J. Andrus: "Revelation and Biblical Authority," *The Calvary Review,* April-June 1963)

Having summarized some arguments for Biblical authority, consider this definition: "Authority is that property by which God demands faith and obedience in all its declarations" (Lorne C. Sanny, "Steering Straight," *Navigator's Log,* date unknown). Stott defines it as "the power or weight which inheres in Scripture because of what it is, namely, a divine revelation given by divine inspiration. If it is a word from God, it has authority over men" (Stott, *op. cit.*).

Perhaps an obvious answer to the question of why the Bible is authoritative is the matter of its origin. "We are to accept the rule of Scripture over our thoughts, because God is its Primary Author. That fact alone gives the Bible its objective authority and nothing must be allowed to dispute its claim." (Douglas Johnson: *The Christian and His Bible,* p. 144)

The same writer refers to the statement of the Westminster Confession of Faith: "The authority of the Holy Scripture, for which it ought to be believed and obeyed, dependeth not upon the testimony of any man or church, but wholly upon God (who is truth itself), the author thereof; and therefore, it is to be received, because it is the Word of God" (chapter 1, section iv).

We used to say that a man's word was his bond. A man's word is only as good as his character. God's Word, then, is as good as God Himself—as dependable, as authoritative as He. If He is the supreme authority—and He is—then His Word is supreme authority. One final testimony to that supreme authority is the testimony of Jesus Christ. Jesus Christ was (is) God, the second person of the Trinity. Surely, His attitude toward the Scriptures is significant, and it is clearly revealed in the accounts of His life. This attitude might be summarized in these statements:

1. He had not come to abolish the law and the prophets (Matt. 5:17ff).
2. He said David was inspired by the Holy Spirit (Mark 12:36).
3. He attributed Moses' statement about marriage in Genesis to God (Matt. 19:4-5).
4. He answered temptation with Scripture (Matt. 4:4, 7, 10).
5. He answered questions with Scripture (Luke 10:25, 26ff).
6. He accused some of misusing it (examples: Mark 7:1-13; 12:18-27).
7. He endorsed the Old Testament as the Word of God and submitted to its authority. (See chapters 2 and 4.)
8. He foresaw the writing of the New Testament and made provision for it by appointing and authorizing His apostles. (See chapters 2 and 4.)

(Stott, *op. cit.*)

B. How it is authoritative. It is often said that the Bible is not a history book or a science book; therefore, we do not go to it as a primary source for the study of history or science. Our study in chapter 4, however, will cause us to conclude that where the Bible speaks in regard to history or science, it can (must) be received as correct. It must be acknowledged, however, that God did not give the Scriptures primarily for the purpose of teaching such things. It does have supreme historical value, of course. However, it was not given merely to provide an authentic and dependable record, but to present God's message; and it does so with fidelity to fact and with forcefulness. The difference in the authority of the Bible as opposed to that of a science textbook or even a political constitution is in the fact that it comes from God.

Where does the authority of the United States Constitution lie? In the government that authored and enforces it (ultimately, the people who support it). But, the Scriptures are from God Himself; He authored them, fulfills them, performs their pronouncements.

The Bible's authority, moreover, extends beyond its reliability as a record of events in history. It is authoritative *now* as a voice from God. It is not static, but dynamic. It is the revelation by which God still speaks today. It is relevant and powerful in the lives of those who receive it and obey its teachings.

One might well ask, "Is the Bible a source book for every life situation and circumstance?" The answer is yes and no. The Bible does not offer full and complete knowledge on every conceivable subject. It does not give rules or examples for every area of life. So, there are matters which aren't even discussed in the Scriptures, and there are other matters which are not treated with any great detail. For example, what kind of dress did the apostles wear? What were the hair styles of the first century? What did Jesus look like? Apparently, though there are correct answers to these questions, they are not important enough for God to have revealed the answers.

But the Bible does establish principles by which decisions can be made concerning any area of practical concern for the believer.

The matter of the Bible's authority is of great importance to the Christian. He need not debate about his response to God's Word. Like Samuel of old, he must say, "Speak, Lord; for thy servant heareth" (I Sam. 3:9). With that approach to the Bible, he will demonstrate his readiness to do what God wants him to do. Submission to God's Word is fundamental to the Christian; he cannot be a faithful disciple without obedience to the Word; he cannot be a reliable witness apart from the Word. And, finally, for the Christian, the authority of the Bible comes from two sources in combination: a knowledge of its content, and a vital, present tense experience with its author. If he knows the Word, he will recognize its authority and its scope; and, when he is living in a vital relationship with his Saviour, he will respond to the Word in loving obedience.

III. The Bible Is Sufficient for the Christian

Everyone has an authority to which he appeals for final judgment. It may be a philosophy which intrigues him, a political persuasion which captivates him, a social doctrine which motivates him, a religious experience or doctrine which seems to meet his need; or, it may be within himself that he finds his final authority (remember the Judges passages referred to earlier). When called into question about character or conduct, every man needs to be able to answer with the basis of what he believes. What is the source of his motivation? What are his basic assumptions in life?

All religions take root in some authority. Whether it's a guru, a self-proclaimed "messiah," a recognized preacher, a book, or a church, we all have some authority upon which we base our religious beliefs and practices. The Bible has been that authority for orthodox Christianity from the very beginning. The prophets wrote "Thus saith the Lord" or "The word of the Lord came unto me, saying." New Testament writers penned, "It is written." Billy Graham shouts out, "The Bible says." All of these voices are speaking with authority, and they are finding their authority in an absolute source—the voice of God, or the Scriptures, the written Word of God.

A. The purpose of the Bible. God gave His Word to reveal Himself and His purposes to mankind. His revelation (in the Scriptures) is sufficient for the reader or hearer to know all that is necessary. Consider some of the purposes which the Scripture reveals about itself:

John 20:31 — "These are written, *that ye might believe* that Jesus is the Christ, the Son of God; and that believing, *ye might have life* through his name."

I Corinthians 10:11 — "Now all these things happened unto them for ensamples: and they are *written for our admonition* . . . . "

II Timothy 3:16-17 — "All scripture is given by inspiration of God, and is profitable *for doctrine, for reproof, for correction, for instruction in righteousness: That* the man of God *may be perfect,* throughly *furnished* unto all good works."

I John 1:4 — "These things write we unto you, *that your joy may be full."*

I John 2:1 — "These things write I unto you, *that ye sin not* . . . . "

I John 5:13 — "These things have I written unto you . . . *that ye may know* that ye have eternal life . . . . "

B. The scope of the Bible. The list above is incomplete, of course, but consider its breadth. Everything necessary for a man to gain eternal life, progress in the Christian life, be equipped for service, come to maturity, and so on, is all included in the Scriptures. Nothing we need for successful Christian living is omitted. We need nothing more, in terms of revelation from God, than what we already have. The Scriptures are sufficient.

Note some of the references which indicate the importance and scope of the Scriptures for the believer:

We are born again by the Word (I Peter 2:3)

We grow by the Word (I Peter 2:2)

Faith comes by hearing the Word (Romans 10:17)

We are sanctified by the Word (John 17:17)

Jesus said to "Search the scriptures . . . they are they which testify of me" (John 5:39)

The writer of Acts commends the Bereans: "These were more noble . . . in that they received the word with all readiness of mind, and searched the scriptures daily, whether those things were so" (Acts 17:11)

Since the Bible is divine and authoritative, we need no other authority; in fact, there could be none. Therefore, we must set a guard about us that we neither seek nor accept extra-Biblical revelations that may be offered to us. The Mormon has the writings of Joseph Smith, the Christian Scientist the works of Mary Baker Eddy, the Roman Catholic the pronouncements of the Pope, and on and on. All would accept the Bible as inspired of God and as a revelation of God, but they are unwilling to grant its completeness and sufficiency. God has spoken to their prophet, and his writing or teaching is to be considered along with the Bible as authoritative.

The error of that position, however, is easily exposed. Whenever a contradiction is seen between the Bible and the extra-Biblical revelation, or whenever greater clarity is desired in application to life, it is not the Bible that is appealed to for final decision. Rather, the Bible must always submit to the "later revelation"—be it the Pope or some prophet. If the Bible is not final authority, obviously it is not authoritative at all. You cannot have both!

The concluding verses of the Scripture make this plain, too:

If any man shall add unto these things, God shall add unto him the plagues that are written in this book: And if any man shall take away from the words of the book of this prophecy, God shall take away his part out of the book of life, and out of the holy city, and from the things which are written in this book (Rev. 22:18-19).

2

The Marvels of the Bible

I. Uniqueness
   A. Its survival
   B. Its unity
   C. Its harmony

II. Content and Construction
   A. Subject matter
   B. Prophecy
   C. Continuity
   D. Central theme

III. Influence
   A. Audience
   B. Circulation
   C. Influence

Enough has doubtless been said already in this study to demonstrate that the Bible is a marvelous book. Before we look more closely at some of its marvels, perhaps it would be helpful to explain the name we most commonly use in reference to God's written Word.

"Bible" comes from the Greek word meaning books. Daniel 9:2 in the Greek version referred to the Old Testament prophetic writings as "the books." Writers of the apocryphal books occasionally referred to some of the canonical books as "the holy books" (I Maccabees 12:9) or "the rest of the books" (prologue to Ecclesiasticus). In the Christian era, the same terminology was used (II Clement 14:2) and the whole Scriptures were thus referred to by the fifth century. By the thirteenth century, "the Books" became simply "the Book." The evolution of the term, "the Bible" from the plural to the singular concept is providential, stressing the *unity* of the 66 books which are its parts. (Material from *Unger's Bible Handbook,* p. 1)

I. Uniqueness

There is no other book in all of world literature like the Bible. Without doubt, more books have been written about this one Book than about any other volume in the world. Such widespread and universal interest in the Bible, by both scholar and layman, is enough to demonstrate that it is something more than any other literary piece can claim to be.

A. Its survival. Not only is the Bible universally recognized and revered, it is unique in that, like few other writings, it has been widely attacked; and, more than any other, it has been the object of repeated attempts to utterly destroy it. It has outlasted, however, the opposition of critics and all efforts to exterminate it. One of the more fanciful attempts to discredit the Bible was made by Julian, nephew and successor of Constantine the Great. He understood the Bible to teach that Jerusalem would not be rebuilt until the times of the Gentiles were fulfilled (Luke 21:24). To prove that prophecy false, he sent out a crew of men to rebuild the city, so determined was his opposition to the Word of God. But, during the rebuilding effort, a fire broke out of the ruins, the men were destroyed, and the venture was stopped.

Diocletian, the Roman Emperor, in A.D. 303 began the worst attack on the Bible ever known. Almost every Bible was destroyed, and multitudes of Christians died. In the Middle Ages, the ruling church opposed the Bible; those who adhered to it and loved it were hounded and persecuted. It was withheld from the common people. In fact, Martin Luther was a grown man before he ever saw a Bible. His colleague, Carlstadt, had earned his Doctor of Theology degree without ever having read the Bible.

In more recent centuries, opposition to the Bible has been less violent, but no more subtle. Rationalists, liberals, and infidels in the nineteenth century made intellectual assaults against the Bible. Voltaire declared that in 100 years the Bible would not be found except as an antiquarian curiosity, yet the British and Foreign Bible Society utilized a Bible house on the very spot where Voltaire made that brash statement. That house sent out Scriptures by the thousands.

Today, the attack against Scripture is often scientific. The word "science" means "knowledge," and since God is the source of all knowledge, could there really be any disagreement between science and the Bible, God's Word? When all the facts are in—and to be sure there have been many premature pronouncements by the scientists—the Bible will be seen again to have survived the attack.

B. Its unity. Perhaps the clearest indication of the Bible's uniqueness is its unity. When you realize that its 66 books were written by 40 or more human authors over a period of more than 15 centuries, involving at least 3 languages, being penned in several different countries and cultures, and covering a wide variety of subjects, one must indeed marvel at its unity. Think for a moment of the human writers who came from different stations in life and varying cultures.

David and Solomon were kings; Isaiah was a statesman and

a prophet; Peter, James and John were untrained fishermen; Zechariah and Jeremiah were priests as well as prophets; Amos was a herdsman and dresser of sycamore trees; Luke was a highly intelligent, cultured physician; Matthew was a tax collector; and Paul was a colossal scholar. (Charles L. Feinberg: "Is the Bible God's Word or Man's?" p. 3) Could you expect any harmony among the writings of men from such diverse positions in life? No, but it's there!

In a little pamphlet called "History, Facts, and Worth of the Bible," the New York Bible Society lists seven great marks which attest to the unity of the Scriptures: The Bible is one book.

1. From Genesis the Bible bears witness to *one God*. Wherever He speaks or acts, He is consistent with Himself, and with the total revelation concerning Him.

2. The Bible forms *one continuous story*—the story of humanity in relation to God.

3. The Bible hazards the most unlikely *predictions* concerning the future, and, when the centuries have brought around the appointed time, records their fulfillment.

4. The Bible is a *progressive* unfolding of truth. Nothing is told all at once and once for all. The law is "first the blade, then the ear, and after that the full corn." Without the possibility of collusion, often with centuries between, one writer of Scripture takes up an earlier revelation, adds to it, lays down the pen, and in due time another man moved by the Holy Spirit, and another, and another, adds details till the whole is complete.

5. From the beginning to the end, the Bible testifies to *one redemption*.

6. From beginning to end, the Bible has *one great theme*—the person and work of the Christ.

7. And, finally, these writers, some 44 in number, writing through 20 centuries, have produced a *perfect harmony* of doctrine in progressive unfolding. (pp. 13-16)

C. Its harmony. The unity of the Bible suggests a related unique quality, its harmony, just referred to. Some seem to think that the Bible is full of contradictions and that its parts are even contradictory. The Old Testament teaches law and judgment while the New reveals grace, love, and salvation, for example. Careful study, however, will reveal the truth of the following statements as to the Bible's continuity and harmony:

The New Testament is in the Old Testament concealed.

The Old Testament is in the New Testament revealed.

The New Testament is in the Old Testament contained.

The Old Testament is in the New Testament explained.

The New Testament is in the Old Testament enfolded.

The Old Testament is in the New Testament unfolded.

The harmony of the Scriptures can be seen in the various manners in which the central theme is woven throughout the fabric of the 66 books. See below for further discussion of the Bible's central theme. Here we'll simply state the theme to be God's plan of redemption for sinful men made possible by the sacrificial death of His Son.

II. Content and Construction

A. Subject matter. The subject matter of the Bible is as varied as the background of its writers. It deals with the broad subjects of man's maker, his destiny, and his present life. It doesn't record what man thinks about these things, but what God has to say to man about them. The Bible reveals His attitude toward sin and its consequences, His justice and mercy, and love, and the person and work of His Son. But the subjects of the Bible are not only religious. A listing of the topics of the Bible might include: history, philosophy, medicine, law, geography, astronomy, religion, psychology, political science, and physiology. The types of literature in its pages are varied, too, and include poetry, drama, biography, prophecy, sermons, conversations, monologues, parables, and various figures of speech.

Although the Bible is not a science book, nor a history

book, nor a psychology or drama book, whenever it includes these things, it is a masterpiece!

B. Prophecy. One of the subjects in the Bible is prophecy, or, perhaps we could put it better by saying that one of the forms of expression used frequently in the Bible is prophecy. The Scriptures don't talk about prophecy so much as they merely prophesy. That is, the writers record God's revelation of events oftentimes far in advance of the actual occurrence. The amazing fulfillment of many of these prophecies hundreds of years after their utterance is another marvel of the Book which testifies to its divine origin and inspiration! Those prophecies which have not been fulfilled do not disprove the Bible, for there is not a single one that cannot yet be fulfilled. Predictions of the coming of Christ were either fulfilled at His first advent (Christmas) or will be at His second advent (the rapture of the church followed by His revelation when He comes to establish His kingdom here on earth).

C. Continuity. Consider again the continuity of the Bible. See the statements above describing the relationship of the Old Testament to the New. Remembering that the Bible is one book, let us also note that the Bible is a book of books.

Sixty-six books make up the one Book. Considered with reference to the unity of the one book, the separate books may be regarded as chapters. But that is but one side of the truth, for each of the 66 books is complete in itself and has its own theme and analysis. It is therefore of the utmost moment that the books be studied in the light of their distinctive themes. Genesis, for instance, is the book of beginnings—the seed-plot of the whole Bible. Matthew is the book of the King, etc. (New York Bible Society, pp. 16-17)

There will be more about individual books and their themes in later chapters. Note here that the Bible's books fall into groups. There are five great divisions in the Scriptures, relative to the one theme of Christ:

1. The Old Testament relates the *preparation* for Christ.

2. The Gospels are the *manifestation* of Christ to the world.
3. The Acts relates the *propagation* of Christ and the Gospel throughout the world.
4. The epistles are the *explanation* of Christ and His Gospel.
5. The Revelation is the *consummation;* all the purposes of God are consummated in Christ.

D. Central theme. Let's return to the matter of the Bible's central theme. This is what ties it all together and makes the marvel of its unity so unique and outstanding! The central theme of the Bible is Christ. It is the manifestation of Jesus Christ, "God manifest in the flesh" (I Tim. 3:16), His sacrificial death, and His resurrection—all of which constitute the Gospel. All preceding Scripture pointed to this, and all following Scripture proceeds from it. The Gospel is preached in the Book of Acts and explained in the epistles. Christ is revealed as the son of God, the son of man, the son of Abraham, and the son of David; and He thus binds the many books into one Book. Seed of the woman (Gen. 3:15), He is the ultimate destroyer of Satan; seed of Abraham, He is the world blesser; seed of David, He is Israel's king. Exalted to the right hand of God, He is "head over all things to the church, which is his body, ... " (Eph. 1:22-23) while to Israel and to the nations the promise of His return forms the one and only rational expectation that humanity will yet fulfill itself. To Him, the Holy Spirit throughout this gospel age bears testimony. The last book of all, the consummation book, is "The Revelation of Jesus Christ" (Rev. 1:1). (New York Bible Society, p. 21)

III. Influence

A. Audience. While it cannot be said that every human being on earth has had the opportunity to see a Bible, it is true that the Bible has universal appeal. Neither age, location, culture, sex, nor any other factor—other than sin and one's refusal to read it—diminishes the appeal and effect of the

Scriptures. All other books have limited appeal in terms of interest and even less value in terms of permanent effect.

Van Dyke describes this wide appeal in a reading from "Our Daily Bread":

> The Bible comes into the palace to tell the monarch that he is a servant of the Most High, and into the cottage to assure the peasant that he is a son of God! Children listen to its stories with wonder and delight, and wise men ponder them as parables of life. The Bible has a word of peace for the time of peril, and a word of light for the hour of darkness. The wicked and the proud tremble at its warnings, but to the wounded and penitent it has a mother's voice. It has woven itself into our deepest dreams so that love, friendship, sympathy, and devotion, memory and hope put on the beautiful garments of its treasured speech, breathing its frankincense and myrrh. No man is poor or desolate who has this treasure for his own. When the landscape darkens and the trembling pilgrim comes to the valley of the shadow, he is not afraid to enter. He takes the rod and staff of Scripture in his hand and says to his friends and comrades, "Goodby, we shall meet again." Comforted by that support, he walks through momentary darkness into eternal light.

B. Circulation. The Bible is centuries old, the completed Old and New Testaments date back nearly 1,900 years. It has been printed in hundreds of languages, and multiplied millions of copies have been printed and distributed. It remains a best seller, year after year. Parts of it appear in nearly every corner of the world, even behind the Iron and Bamboo curtains. Men have willingly sacrificed their lives in its translation, manufacture, and distribution.

C. Influence. In the words of Charles Feinberg:

> No book has its [the Bible's] power to change men from sinners to saints, from bestiality to blessedness, from vice to virtue, from greed to godliness, from the pit to His presence, from hell to heaven .... Many books can make wise unto mathematics, the social sciences, the natural sciences, and the philosophies, but only one Book has ever been able to make one wise *unto salvation*—the Bible! (Feinberg, *op. cit.*, p. 13)

Testimonies to the influence and value of the Bible are too numerous to give a very comprehensive coverage, but here are just a few:

The most learned, acute, and diligent student can not, in the longest life, obtain an entire knowledge of this one volume. The more deeply he works the mine, the richer and more abundant he finds the ore; new light continually beams from this source of heavenly knowledge, to direct the conduct and illustrate the work of God and the ways of men; and he will at least leave the world confessing that the more he studied the Scriptures, the fuller conviction he had of his own ignorance, and of their inestimable value. (Sir Walter Scott)

There never was found, in any age of the world, either in religion or law that did so highly exalt the public good as the Bible. (Bacon)

All the good from the Savior of the world is communicated through this Book; but for this Book we could not know right from wrong. All the things desirable to man are contained in it. (Abraham Lincoln)

We can summarize the theme of this chapter by presenting the outline of the introductory chapter in Irving L. Jensen's book, *Enjoy Your Bible.*

1. The Bible is a miracle book as to its *birth.*
2. The Bible is a miracle book as to its 66 individual books gradually *growing* into one unit.
3. The Bible is a miracle book as to its *transmission* through the thousands of scribal copyings into the modern printing era.
4. The Bible is a miracle book as to its very *survival* through all the centuries.
5. The Bible is a miracle book as to its world-wide *reception* and *influence.*

The Word of the Living God is "supernatural in origin; eternal in duration; inexpressible in value; infinite in scope; divine in authorship; human in penmanship; regenerative in power; infallible in authority; universal in interest; personal in application; and as St. Paul declares, inspired in totality." (Canon Hague, quoted by Feinberg, *op. cit.,* p. 15)

3

How God Gave the Bible

In chapter 1 it was mentioned that the Bible reveals God; in fact, it is His self-revelation. What do we mean by "revelation"? How did God actually reveal Biblical truth? Another word you'll find often in discussions of the Bible is "inspiration." What do we mean by "inspiration"? In what sense is the Bible inspired? It is the purpose of this chapter to answer these questions briefly and in simple terms. Look to the theology books for technical treatments of these subjects.

I. Revelation

A. What is revelation? We recognize that the word itself has to do with bringing something into the open that has previously been obscured or hidden. Dr. Alva J. McClain, first president of Grace Theological Seminary, taught that "Revelation is God's activity in communicating truth to the human mind." Another defines it thus: "Revelation is the communicating of truth which otherwise could not be known."

If we examine these definitions, we discover these elements: communication—communication to humans; communication of truth; communication of what had been previously unknown; communication of what God wants men to know. God has revealed what He wants us to know, and what He has revealed is the truth.

What is involved in this revelation? What kind of material is included in the Bible? If you've read the Bible at all, you will recognize that there is a great deal of historical data included in its pages. Specific events, places, and people are mentioned frequently. Many can be verified by secular history, but others may have to be accepted on the evidence of the Word of God only. Secondly, the Bible records many personal experiences. Events in the lives of real, live people and families are related. Abraham, Moses, Daniel, Joseph, Jesus, Paul—the list goes on and on; many of their intimate and social activities and thoughts are shared. Most of them would not be known if it were not for their inclusion in the Scriptures.

More significant, however, is the third type of material

included in the Bible: direct revelation. Frequently, God spoke to men—whether face to face or in visions and dreams (see below)—and unfolded truths to them that were entirely unknown at the time, and impossible to know by any human agency or source. These are the materials that make the Bible a miracle book. Perhaps it should be noted that not everything in the Bible was directly revealed by God. Certain matters were discovered through personal experience or by the accounts of others. As we shall see later, however, though not everything in the Bible came by direct revelation, everything in the Bible is inspired.

To summarize the matter of what revelation is, we quote Douglas Johnson regarding "The essential character of revelation":

> It is important to note that it is as essential to the Bible's view of revelation to emphasize the supernatural nature of the means through which it has been acquired as the supernatural source from which it comes. God has made Himself and His gracious purposes known to man in an immediate and direct Word of God, which is reverently to be received by man. This authoritative message has not been attained by human effort. It must simply be received. In fact, this giving of the revelation and the process of enshrining it in a written record is to be viewed as a part of the redemptive work of God. . . . We must insist, with Professor B. B. Warfield, that "the organs of revelation occupy a receptive attitude. The contents of their messages are not something thought out, inferred, hoped for, or feared by them, but are something conveyed to them, often forced upon them, by the irresistible might of the revealing Spirit." (Douglas Johnson: *The Christian and His Bible,* pp. 43-44)

B. How did revelation take place? Granted that God revealed truth to the writers of Scripture. That's what revelation means. But how did He do it? Many writers have listed the methods used in revelation. We'll enumerate 10, some of which may overlap others. God revealed truth through:

1. Personal experience. A good example is Psalm 51. In

the difficult experience of his rebellion and sin and the subsequent confession and forgiveness, David is able to write about these matters and, in so doing, reveal precious truth which God intends men to have.

2. The writing of God. In Exodus 31:18 and 32:16 it is indicated that God Himself wrote on tables of stone: " . . . two tables of testimony, tables of stone, written with the finger of God"; "And the tables were the work of God, and the writing was the writing of God, graven upon the tables."

3. The interpretation of dreams. Fascinating stories are told about men of God who interpreted dreams. Read of Joseph in Genesis 40 and 41 or of Daniel in chapters 2 and 4 of his prophecy. Future events were foretold in the dreams, and their interpretation revealed, in some cases, history pre-written many centuries in advance.

4. Interpretation of miracles. In Daniel 5, a startling miracle occurred. Witnessed by a crowd of party-goers, a hand wrote upon the wall. Daniel interpreted that miracle and handwriting, revealing truth that God wanted the nation to hear. (Since then, the expression "the handwriting on the wall" has become commonplace to describe impending failure or defeat.)

5. Personal dreams. Again, Daniel is an example. The marvelous prophecy of the 70 weeks, recorded in Daniel 7, explains and enlarges on the prophetic timetable that Daniel had been researching.

6. Visions. Whether in dreams or not, both Daniel (chap. 8) and Ezekiel (Ezek. 1:1) are said to have received truth from God through visions. So did other writers; John, for example, in Revelation chapter 1, though his experience is not named a vision there.

7. Messages by angels. Angels appeared to Daniel (chap. 9); to Joseph, Mary's betrothed (Matt. 1:20-21); to Zacharias, the priest and father of John the Baptist (Luke 1:

11-20); and to Mary (Luke 1:26-38), to mention but four.

8. The Spirit of the Lord. No doubt, these occurrences cannot be separated by any hard line from the instances where we read that God spoke to men (No. 9), but David claims "The Spirit of the Lord spake by me, and his word was in my tongue" (II Sam. 23:2).

9. The direct voice of God. See, for examples, Exodus 24:1; 33:11 (where He spoke with Moses "face to face"), Jeremiah 36:1. It should also be noted that expressions like "God said," and "the Word of the Lord came unto me" occur hundreds and thousands of times. Someone has counted 2,700 such statements in the Old Testament alone.

10. Jesus Christ. God's written word has been revealed, finally, and most clearly and completely, through the living Word, Jesus Christ. He is referred to in John 1 as "the Word."

The 10 means or methods of revelation listed here can be summed up in a single brief passage, Hebrews 1:1-2: "God, after He spoke long ago to the fathers in the prophets in many portions and in many ways, in these last days has spoken to us in His Son. . . . " (NASB).

The key passage in all of Scripture regarding its source and the means of its communication is II Peter 1:15-21. Before the critical twenty-first verse, Peter verifies the New Testament. He indicates that he is not basing his testimony on fables or myths, but he is giving eyewitness accounts. (John and Luke write similarly in I John 1:1 and Luke 1:1-4.) Peter witnessed the coming of Christ—His life, transfiguration, death, resurrection, post-resurrection appearances and ministry, and His ascension—all in fulfillment of Old Testament prophecies.

In verses 19-21, he authenticates the Old Testament, and we should observe some critical truths which he emphasizes. He points out the value of prophecy: it is sure and certain;

it has been confirmed by fulfillment. It is a light. But it is temporary, " . . . until the day dawn, and the day star arise in your hearts" (II Peter 1:19). By the way, the "more sure word of prophecy" is the Scriptures. They are more sure than the very eyewitness accounts which he is able to report. So, until Christ comes, we have a reliable revelation of what God wants us to know.

Verse 21 indicates something of the source and method of revelation. Prophecy (or Scripture) did not come by the will or desire of men. No one ever sat down and determined to write Scripture. Rather, God chose holy men—not just anyone, but men who lived in harmony with His will and plan—and by His Spirit He carried them along in their experiences, gathering of information, and formation of thoughts, so they were able to put down exactly what He wanted to convey to men. That's how revelation took place!

C. The channels of revelation. Finally, consider how God prepared the writers of the Bible. He did not simply dictate to inanimate or unthinking objects; they were neither "Stenorettes" or memory typewriters. They exercised their originality and creativity as influenced by their personalities, training, talents, and environments. But God, nonetheless, prepared them for their work. Paul was conscious of God's preparing him for his ministry. He wrote: "But when it pleased God, who separated me from my mother's womb, and called me by his grace, To reveal his Son in me, that I might preach him among the heathen. . . . " (Gal. 1:15-16). God spoke to Jeremiah in this manner: "Before I formed thee in the belly I knew thee; and before thou camest forth out of the womb I sanctified thee, and I ordained thee a prophet unto the nations" (Jer. 1:5).

God chose men fitted to fulfill His purposes. See some examples:

1. Moses—raised in Pharoah's court (Exod. 2:10) and thus prepared to deal with Egypt's leaders—and later to record the events accurately.

2. David—a practicing shepherd as a lad and young man, ideally suited to write from his experience the beloved twenty-third Psalm. Many other Psalms reflect his experiences as outdoorsman, refugee, soldier, and statesman.

3. Daniel—carried captive to Babylon (Dan. 1:6), educated and trained. He excelled (Dan. 1:19) and became adviser to generations of rulers. Thus, he was able to understand God's revelations to Him and record them for our edification.

4. Paul—read Philippians 3:4-6 and following to see how God revealed to Paul truth that had not been known previously ("mysteries"). He was the ideal recipient of these mysteries because of his training, education, religious zeal, etc.

Paul comments on this theme in II Corinthians 1:3-6 (which read). He points out that his experiences were directed of God for purposes beyond just his own life and need. He was prepared by them to minister to others. What wider ministry has Paul had than to have written such a large portion of the New Testament? Think what a great loss we would experience if we did not have his contribution to the Bible! God prepared His writers and revealed His truth to us through them. That's revelation.

II. Inspiration

Having taken these lengths to discuss the first important term, we cannot slight the other; but, perhaps, we'll be able to touch it a little more briefly.

A. What do we mean by inspiration? This term is more misunderstood, perhaps, than the previous one. Revelation seems to have an obvious meaning. So does inspiration. It is widely used; but in relation to the Scriptures it has a more technical meaning, and that is what we must come to terms with.

As II Peter 1:21 was the key text in our discussion of

revelation, so II Timothy 3:16 is the key passage regarding inspiration: "All scripture is given by inspiration of God. . . ." The word translated inspiration, literally rendered from the Greek New Testament, would be "God-breathed." That says something about the source of Scripture—it comes from God; it is as intimately associated with God as His breath.

Now, this is quite different from the inspiration we refer to when we say that Shakespeare, or Milton, or Shelley, was inspired. Bach, Beethoven, and Brahms may be said to have been inspired, too, but we're not talking about the same thing when we speak of the inspiration of the Bible. For, it is not the *writers* of the Bible who were inspired, but their *writings*. To say an artist is inspired is to imply that he has had some special, strong influence come upon him that enabled him to write, compose, or paint with extraordinary ability. The result of that inspiration is a piece of literature or music, or a picture. What we have may or may not accurately reflect what the artist was inspired to transmit; he may be satisfied or dissatisfied with the product, but he was inspired to produce it.

The point we're trying to make may not yet be clear. Dr. McClain put it this way: "Revelation has to do with the *material*; inspiration with the *record*." Alfred Martin pointed out that "Revelation is the *communicating* of what otherwise could not be known; inspiration is the *recording* of that truth." Perhaps these subtleties may be clarified with a more formal definition: "By the inspiration of the Holy Spirit, God supernaturally directed the writers of Scripture . . . [so that] God's own complete and coherent message to men was recorded in perfect accuracy . . . . " (John Walvoord).

A final thought should be noted. Inspiration applies only to the original writing, and it must be acknowledged that all the original documents are now lost. This problem will be studied in chapter 5.

B. Other terms relating to inspiration. Three or four other words appear frequently in discussions of the inspiration of the Bible, and these are significant and should be understood.

1. Verbal—verbal inspiration simply means that the very words of the Bible are inspired, not just ideas or thoughts, but the specific words that appeared in the original writings. In I Corinthians 2:13, Paul seems clearly to emphasize this truth: "Which things also we speak, not in the words which man's wisdom teacheth, but which the Holy Ghost teacheth . . . ." John Stott comments: "Nor is this in the least surprising, for it is not possible to convey a precise message in any other way than in precise words."

2. Plenary or full—the whole Bible, all of Scripture, is equally inspired by God. "To say that all Scripture is inspired of God (II Tim. 3:16) is to say that all Scripture is the direct product of the creative breath of God" (Alva J. McClain). As was noted earlier, not everything in the Bible was directly revealed, but it was all inspired. The record is certain and sure.

3. Inerrant—the Bible is free from mistakes. If, indeed, it is the Word of God, it is as dependable as God Himself. It could not be His product and contain error. (Remember, we're making this claim for the original documents; as for the translations we now use and their inerrancy, see chapter 4.)

4. Infallible—this term is virtually the same as "inerrant" with just a bit more strength. Inerrant means without error; infallible means that it is not able to be wrong. Again, note that it is not the writers who were infallible; for they were capable of error. Many demonstrated that sad fact. But it is the writings that are infallible. God could not breathe out anything but truth; it could not contain error and be His product.

Lest this final matter of infallibility be misunderstood, we hasten to make a statement that may sound like we reject the last two points listed. Some things in the Bible are not true. Did you get that? We believe in the inerrancy and infallibility of the Bible, but some things in the Bible are not true. Hear us out. Some of the conclusions of Job's friends are not true. Satan's words are sometimes half-truths or outright lies, yet they are recorded in the Bible. The Psalmist quotes a fool who says, "There is no God" (Psalm 14:1) but that's a lie! If you will recall that inspiration has to do with the record, you can see that this doctrine guarantees us that we have an accurate record. The Bible correctly records the false conclusions of Job's friends, the lies of Satan, the blasphemous error of the fool, and so forth. The Scripture clearly refutes these philosophical and theological errors when they occur, but they are accurately recorded for our edification.

C. Proofs of inspiration. Space does not permit us to refute various false theories of inspiration which abound today. If we understand the truth, we ought not be confused by error, so perhaps we can concentrate on the positive and omit mentioning the negative. (For a concise, clear, and helpful treatment of several false theories, refer to a personal Bible study guide from Moody Press by Alfred and Dorothy Martin titled *The Bible*.)

Again, we haven't space to give an exhaustive or comprehensive treatment of the proofs of inspiration, but we will list a few:

1. The testimony of Jesus Christ. Jesus verified the Old Testament writings, quoting from every portion of them. He also authenticated the New Testament, foreseeing its production and preparing for it.

2. The testimony of the Bible writers. The human agents of both the Old and New Testaments were conscious of the fact they were recording "God's Word." Their language often reflects that truth (Isaiah 1:10; Jeremiah 1:2, et al.).

3. Fulfilled prophecy. Prophecies about Christ, the nation of Israel, the Church, world conditions—so many have been fulfilled in such great detail that only the Bible's inspiration could account for the phenomenon.

4. Archeological discoveries. All over Bible lands, the diggings of scholars have repeatedly confirmed the Bible writings. When secular searchers find new evidence, it invariably supports what has already been revealed by the Scriptures.

5. Christian experience. Whoever has "tasted" of the Bible and responded in faith to its precepts can testify to its truth, accuracy, and benefit.

Let's conclude our discussion of inspiration by quoting a question and answer which appeared in *Encounter* magazine some time ago. John A. Caiger responds to the question, "What is the use today of upholding the verbal inspiration of the Scripture in view of the fact that the originally inspired Scriptures are lost (and therefore cannot be consulted) and instead of the original Scriptures we have hundreds of different readings?"

The reason why we must uphold the doctrine of the verbal inspiration of the Scriptures is that *the Scriptures teach it*. And since the original documents have perished (which is not at all surprising), Christian scholars are challenged by this doctrine to the greatest possible diligence in their work of discovering what is the purest and most accurate text of the Scriptures.

You rightly speak of hundreds of different copies with their variant readings, but far too much can be made of this. It has been said again and again by the most reputable scholars that all the differences which occur in the various manuscripts do not affect the meaning of a single doctrine. The Gospel stands revealed in the testimony of the Scripture as a whole—it does not depend upon the precise rendering of any one particular text.

We certainly have in our best translations and versions the Scriptures substantially as God breathed them into the minds and lips of His servants, and it is this tremendous truth which gives the stamp of Divine authority to the Bibles we read and use.

Well, there they are—revelation and inspiration. Do you have some understanding now of these terms? It's important that you recognize the Scriptures as the authoritative Word of God. The Bible is authoritative simply because it is God's

Word. He said it, so it's true. It's true, so we must accept it and act upon it. Whether or not we understand the particulars of these matters, whether or not we can explain them, we are obligated to respond to the authoritative Word from God! Isn't it wonderful to know that He has spoken, and we have the record of what He has said in His Word!

4

The Reliability of the Bible

I. The Canon
   A. What is the canon?
   B. How did the 66 books come to be included in the canon?

II. Reliability
   A. Attested content
   B. Reliability illustrated

III. Inerrancy
   A. The true
   B. The false

Can the Bible be depended upon? Is it reliable? Certainly, every Christian wants to have a dependable word from God. However, it is in this very area that the Scriptures are being undercut today in some sectors of evangelicalism because of new interpretations of inerrancy or infallibility. These terms were discussed in the preceding chapter where they were defined as: inerrancy—the quality of being without error, free from mistakes; infallibility—the quality of not being able to be wrong. These terms will need some expansion; an understanding of them will add to our confidence in the Bible as the Word of God.

Also, when we realize that the 66 books we have in our Bible are exactly the 66 God intended us to have—no more and no less—we appreciate, again, its reliability.

I. The Canon

The term "the canon" is generally used among orthodox Christians to refer to the 66 books of the Bible—39 in the Old Testament and 27 in the New. The scholarly research which pursues the subject of which books are to be included in the Bible is called textual criticism. It is not our purpose here to go into great detail, but the interested student can follow his interest in studying this subject in a good library on Biblical studies.

A. What is the canon? This little word comes from the Greek language, in which it originally referred to a measuring rod. Later, it meant the rule by which the basic teaching of the Christian faith was to be known; in other words, it defined a group of doctrines. Finally, it came to refer to the completed catalog of books in the New Testament. Today, we use it in speaking of the catalog of books in both the Old and New Testaments.

Another way of understanding the term is to remember its original meaning as a measuring rod; it was the rule by which each book of the Bible was tested before receiving recognition as a genuine part of the Bible. Finally, it came to be the name for the collection of books which came up to the standard.

It must be noted, however, that men do not determine what is God's Word and what is not; the most they can do (or have done) is recognize what is inherently authoritative and inspired. More about that later, but let us just say here that it is not the canon that makes a book authoritative; the 66 books of the Bible were already authoritative because they were God's Word even before they were recognized formally as such.

B. How did the 66 books come to be included in the canon? There are several tests, referred to as "tests of canonicity," which have been used to judge the merit of writings purporting to be from God. The late Dr. L. L. Grubb listed four:

1. Divine authorship. Is it inspired? Was it given by God through men moved by the Holy Spirit, or is it from man alone?
2. Human authorship. Was it written by a prophet, apostle, or other spokesman for God?
3. Genuineness. Can it be traced back to the time and writer from whom it professes to come? If the writer is uncertain, does the content of the book contain the same matter as when it was written?
4. Authenticity. Is it a true record of actual facts and circumstances?

(L. L. Grubb: Notes on "The Development of the Bible")

Dr. Grubb concluded by saying that the first two tests are sufficiently strong to settle the matter of the canonicity of any book qualifying to be a part of the Bible.

Douglas Johnson summarizes the subject well in these two quotes:

It is primarily upon the ground of its inherent authority that the main stream of orthodoxy in the Christian church has based, and must base, its claim for the canon of Scripture. (p. 62)

In the final analysis, the Christian argument for the Canon rests squarely on a basic conviction. It is that, in the context of the Being of God and of His revelation of Himself in Christ (mediated to us through patriarch, prophet, and apostle), we possess in Holy Scripture a body of divinely authoritative and self-authenticating documents.

(Douglas Johnson: *The Christian and His Bible,* p. 71)

There have been other writings, of course, that men have put forth as words from God. In early centuries, some were given consideration, but none received widespread recognition as being inherently authoritative. Most widely known of these writings is a collection of 14 books, or parts of books, known as the apocrypha. The word itself originally meant "concealed" or "hidden," likely used because these writings were associated with groups, often heretical sects, which were not a part of the mainstream of Judaism. The term later bore the meaning of spurious or fraudulent.

The apocryphal books are strikingly dissimilar to the recognized books of the Bible in terms of their content and literary quality. They include fanciful stories, factual inaccuracies, and morality in contradiction to the inspired books of the Bible. They do include some helpful material, however—especially in the final two books, I and II Maccabees, which cover the 400-year period of history between the Old and New Testament revelations.

In the early centuries of the Christian era, many other apocryphal books appeared, with claims that they were the writings of the apostles. They are to the New Testament what the 14 books of the apocrypha were to the Old. While they may or may not include some factual material, they do not merit consideration as inspired revelation from God. Much of their content relates incidents supposedly from the childhood of Jesus—a period of time virtually unmentioned in the 27 books of the New Testament or in secular history. A number of these writings, by the way, are grouped in what is called the pseudepigrapha. That strange-looking and strange-sounding term means "false writings." They are not what they claim to be and, consequently, are not inspired or authoritative.

II. Reliability

The canon can be relied on; it represents what God wanted us to have in the Bible. Although we do not have the original manuscripts, there is clear evidence that what we have is authentic (See chapter 5 for further treatment of this subject.)

A. Attested content. No literature from antiquity is so well attested as the Bible. There are more than 1,700 manuscripts of the Old Testament and more are being found from time to time in the Middle East (e.g. the Dead Sea Scrolls in 1947 in Qumran which, by the way, confirm the accuracy of the text of Isaiah and other Old Testament passages). Unger says the "New Testament exists in almost 5,000 Greek manuscripts and in more than 10,000 manuscripts which are copies of the early versions. . . . " (*Unger's Bible Handbook*, p. 890)

The Martins add:

> All of these date from the 15th century back toward the time of the original writing. When we realize that of the works of Homer, one of the famous authors of antiquity, there is not a known complete copy of his work earlier than A.D. 1300, we see anew the miracle God performed for His Word.

(Alfred and Dorothy Martin: Personal Study Guide: *The Bible*, p. 36)

After considering all the evidence, we are left with a firm conclusion. In the words of F. F. Bruce, "There is no body of ancient literature in the world which enjoys such a wealth of good textual attestation as the New Testament." (Quoted by Douglas Johnson: *op. cit.*, p. 68)

Although we do not have the "original autographs," the Martins conclude: "The true inspired text of Scripture has not perished but lies in the manuscripts and is represented so carefully and remarkably in the translations, that we need have no fear of missing the voice of God." (Martin, *op. cit.*, p. 37)

B. Reliability illustrated. The reliability of the scriptural accounts is illustrated by the author's introduction to the

Gospel of Luke. In chapter 1, verses 1-4, Luke indicates that he is compiling a record of the events of Christ's life and ministry to aid his addressee, Theophilus, to have "the exact truth" about those matters. He was able to do this, "having investigated everything carefully from the beginning." God used qualified, prepared, capable, and careful men to record His revelation, and they responded with quality workmanship.

In Acts chapter 1, also penned by Luke, he continues his consecutive recording of historical events for the benefit of Theophilus (and us!). Also, consider the writings of Peter and John. Peter talks of his being an eyewitness of the transfiguration of Christ (II Peter 1:16) and John relates " . . . which we have heard, which we have seen with our eyes, which we have looked upon, and our hands have handled. . . ." (I John 1:1). Interestingly enough, though these eyewitness accounts are dependable, Peter says that the Scriptures revealed by God are "a more sure word of prophecy" than even the testimony of eyewitnesses (II Peter 1:19).

In regard to the Old Testament, Irving L. Jensen writes:

> It is a known fact that compared with all other ancient writings, the Old Testament has no close competitor for accuracy of transmission down through the ages. The divine preservation of the text through scribal copyings has been of such a character that by a comparison of the hundreds of extant Old Testament manuscripts a text of the Scriptures can be determined that is substantially pure . . . . Such a claim is not the product of wishful thinking, but the conclusion of hosts of scholars who have devoted their lives to the tasks of textual evaluation and its associated studies.

(Irving L. Jensen: "How Reliable Is Our Present Old Testament Text")

III. Inerrancy

What do we really mean by the statement that the Bible is inerrant, it has no errors in it? In what sense is the Bible without error?

A. The true. The writer accepts unreservedly the traditional, orthodox view of inerrancy; that is, that the Bible is without error in its original autographs or writings (which are nonexistent now). That historical opinion was expressed by B. B. Warfield: "The church has always believed her Scriptures to be the book of God, of which God was in such a sense the author that every one of its affirmations of whatever kind is to be esteemed as the utterance of God, of infallible truth and authority." (B. B. Warfield: *The Inspiration and Authority of the Bible,* p. 112)

The reader must understand that this is the writer's opinion—he is in complete agreement with the foregoing—but he hastens to say that there may very well be errors in the Bible you read in your home or study. These errors fall generally into two kinds:

1. Errors of men that are accurately recorded in Scripture. Men may have lied, made inaccurate judgments, given false teaching; if so, they are recorded in the Bible accurately, but they are, nonetheless, false. Did Satan say to Eve in Genesis 3 that she would not die if she ate of the forbidden fruit? Yes, he did. Does the Bible record that statement? Yes, it does. Is it a correct statement? No, it is a lie. But the Scriptures accurately record that lie. (That's what inspiration is all about—see chapter 3).

2. Errors in translation or textual transmission. When God gave the Scriptures, they were accurate, and the original human authors correctly recorded the revelation. But errors could be—and have been—made in copying the original texts and subsequent copies. Before the age of printing presses (and there are occasional errors in modern printed materials even yet), Scriptures were laboriously copied by hand, letter by letter, word after word. In spite of careful precautions—such as the counting of characters (letters) in a book to be sure the copy had the same number as the original—human errors were made. Numbers might be transposed, for example, or a copyist might insert a phrase at the wrong place. Some-

times, though infrequently, a copyist might interpose a comment—to "help" the reader in his understanding.

All of these errors, however, make a very small number, and none affect any important doctrine of Scripture. You can rest assured that such human mistakes have not altered God's revelation in any significant way.

B. The false. In contrast to the orthodox view of inerrancy is a rather recent view which has created considerable controversy in the Christian world (as well it should!). This view would claim that the Bible is intended to be inerrant only in "revelational" areas; such as the nature of God, salvation, etc., rather than in "non-revelational" areas like geology, cosmology, or botany. In other words, in areas of doctrine God saw to it that the human authors recorded accurately the truth He wanted to give to men. But in areas other than doctrinal, the human authors were left to their own abilities to write; therefore, they may reflect the inaccurate science of their day or give an incorrect historical record.

Arrayed against this new theology is a host of historical and current argument that seems overwhelming to this writer. First, hear another statement of the reknowned author B. B. Warfield whose logic cannot be overlooked: "The authority which cannot assure of a hard fact is soon not trusted for a hard doctrine" (Warfield, *op. cit.,* p. 181). He elsewhere stated: "Revelation is but half revelation unless it be infallibly communicated; it is but half communicated unless it be infallibly recorded" (*Ibid.,* p. 442).

Let's quickly summarize the matter of inerrancy with two more brief quotations: "We believe God's Word to be infallible simply because God Himself is infallible. God is true (John 3:33; 17:3; Romans 3:4; I Thess. 1:9), and since the Scriptures are 'God-breathed' (II Tim. 3:16), they must also be true." (Charles Ryrie: "The Bible: Truth Without Error," p. 4)

"God could never have inspired a human author of Scripture to write anything erroneous or false." (Gleason L.

Archer, Jr. in *Decision,* May 1975)

In the last few years, man's knowledge has increased almost beyond measure. We are told that every few years the total of what is known doubles; in other words, most of what mankind will know in the year 2000 is not known at all today! Fantastic! Knowledge has increased; science has pursued new and startling discoveries; technology has developed appliances, weapons, and gadgets far beyond our wildest imaginations just a short time past.

Amidst all this change in methods, equipment, and knowledge, the Bible declares that "there is nothing new under the sun" (Eccles. 1:9). Every advance in science is but an uncovering of something already existing. Technologists may put things together in new combinations, but God put everything into His creation which is only now being discovered or developed.

Why is it not necessary to have a changing Bible to keep up with the times? Because the Bible deals in unchanging principles. Man is still the same—sinful and rebellious. God is still the same—holy and righteous. The reconciliation of the two is still by the same means—God's gracious provision of salvation received by faith in the redemptive work of Christ.

The Bible does not deal in the passing and transient, but in the eternal and permanent. Though much is said about holy living in the Scriptures, specific sinful practices peculiar to a certain age or location are completely ignored while sins of a universal and age-long character are decried: lying, murder, adultery, etc. Why doesn't the Bible specifically condemn movie-going, smoking, ballroom dancing, acid rock music, and other "sins" of our era? Obviously, such condemnation would not have been understood in the Bible of the first century, much less in Old Testament days. Furthermore, the solid, non-changing principles upon which decisions concerning every facet of conduct can be made are laid down clearly—for men and women of any century or place. The Holy Spirit is able to use the Word to lead the seeking believer to make decisions concerning any practice in life.

If the Bible is without error—as we believe it is—and infallible, then it is trustworthy. It can be relied upon. Do not question its historicity or its scientific accuracy. Continual discoveries in the various sciences serve only to corroborate the revelation God has already given.

If there is any weakness in the Scripture texts we now use, it is in their failure to be studied, applied, and obeyed. It should be the attitude of the Christian to study the Bible, acknowledge its authority and infallibility, confess that it is right and applicable, and obey it wholeheartedly.

"The law of the Lord is *perfect,* converting the soul: the testimony of the Lord is *sure,* making wise the simple. The statutes of the Lord are *right,* rejoicing the heart: the commandment of the Lord is *pure,* enlightening the eyes" (Ps. 19:7-8)

A final comment:

Here in the original Scriptures is something so far above human attainment that a fully adequate translation is well-nigh impossible of achievement. Not one but several versions are needed to bring out anything of the fullness of the simplest New Testament narrative.

When all the heat and dust of controversy as to the "mechanics" of inspiration have subsided, and when the quibblings of the critics as to who wrote what, are forgotten, the Scriptures will remain the unchanging record of God communicating to His creatures, of Christ revealing Himself to His church.

(Herbert Dennett: *A Guide to Modern Versions of the New Testament,* p. vii)

5

How We Got Our Bible

I. Hebrew and Greek Origins
   A. Original languages
   B. Text sources

II. Early History of the English Bible
   A. Septuagint
   B. Vulgate
   C. Early English translations
   D. Wycliffe

III. Versions Leading to the King James
   A. Tyndale
   B. Others
   C. King James

In previous chapters we've discussed how God gave the Bible, the revelation of Himself, to men. That revelation occurred over centuries of time through dozens of men. But how did we get the Bibles we use today in our homes and churches?

I. Hebrew and Greek Origins

Nearly everyone understands that the Bible he holds in his hands is a translation. God did not reveal Himself to mankind in English. When the Holy Spirit moved men to write the Scriptures (II Peter 1:21), they recorded that revelation in the common language of their day.

A. Original languages. Consequently, the Old Testament was written almost entirely in the Hebrew language, the mother tongue of the writers of the Old Testament books. Brief portions of the Old Testament, by the way, were written in Aramaic, the language of Babylon. However, the great bulk of it is in Hebrew.

The New Testament was originally recorded in Greek—not the classical Greek of Aristotle or Homer, nor the modern Greek of today, but what is known as *koine* Greek—common Greek. In preparing for the coming of His Son to earth (in "the fulness of the time"—Gal. 4:4), God saw to it that commerce, government, education—everything—was fully developed for Messiah's appearance. Circumstances were so arranged that His story was able to be spread rapidly throughout the world of that day.

One of the circumstances was the almost universal knowledge of a trade language—*koine* Greek. While people of various nations and tribes spoke their own local languages, there was general knowledge of Greek all around the world. Commerce, industry, and trade could easily be carried on by participants from widely separated places because they knew a common *lingua franca.*

The message of the New Testament, therefore, quickly moved throughout the world and found a ready audience—because its language was almost universally known. It is no accident or mere happenstance of history, then, that the original autographs of sacred Scripture appeared in the languages that they did.

The fact must be faced, however, that we do not possess today a single manuscript of the original writings. That may be a circumstance deplored by some, but it is not so tragic as one might at first assume. After all, the original manuscript of the Emancipation Proclamation was lost in an Ohio fire, but copies of it have preserved the text.

Why don't we have the original manuscripts? "Perhaps the Lord realized that, if we had them, foolish men would worship the *Book* instead of the *Author,* and probably would build shrines to it and make it the occasion for superstition, pagan worship, and idolatry." (Richard DeHaan: *The Book of Books,* pp. 13-14)

Such a tendency might be illustrated by the beautiful museum in Jerusalem today which has been built to commemorate the finding of the Dead Sea Scrolls. It's called the "Shrine of the Book" and its architectural design is unique. It's in the shape of the top of an earthen pot such as the one in which the scrolls were found in Qumran.

Our statement of belief in the inspiration of Scripture refers, of course, to the original writings. We have already acknowledged certain insignificant errors in translation and transmission of the text (see chapter 4). The question arises, then, "how do we know that what we presently have is accurate at all?" As indicated in the previous chapter, what we do have today is quite reliable, and we shall only briefly set down here a summary of evidence. Students interested in a more technical discussion should consult the works of textual critics such as Kenyon, *Textual Criticism of the New Testament;* or F. F. Bruce, *The Book and the Parchments.*

B. Text sources. The best of our Bibles today is based on careful study of thousands of documents. There are three sources for our Bible texts:

1. Manuscripts—as the word itself suggests, these are hand-

written copies of the books of the Bible, made from the original writings which are now all gone, as far as we know.

2. Versions—these are translations—either of the original manuscripts or of other versions. For example, the Septuagint is a version; it is a translation into Greek of the original Hebrew manuscripts.

3. The Fathers—in the writings of the early Church Fathers are some 86,000 quotations of references to Scripture (reference is from *Unger's Bible Handbook*, p. 891).

Our earliest manuscripts take us back to the second century A.D., but the writings of the early Church Fathers bridge the gap between that point and the ancient writings of the New Testament.

Much of the Old Testament, and practically all of the New Testament, could be reproduced from the writings of the Fathers. An English scholar is reported to have searched these writings and claimed to have found all but 11 verses.

The Fathers are too numerous to name here, but the following list with brief comments for some will demonstrate the importance of their contributions in determining the proper Biblical text:

Clement of Rome—a contemporary of the Apostle John; his "First Epistle to the Corinthians," ca. A.D. 96, is a valuable piece of literature and was thought by some to be worthy of inclusion in the New Testament. In it he quoted from 12 New Testament books.

Ignatius

Polycarp

Irenaeus—a student of Polycarp who was a student of John

Justin Martyr—quoted largely from the Old Testament, but also from eight New Testament books

Clement of Alexander—used 2,400 New Testament quotations and quoted from all but two Old Testament books and all but three in the New Testament

Tertullian—quoted *THE* in New Testament 7,200 times—3,800 from the Gospels

Cyprian—used 750 Old Testament quotations and 1,030 New Testament quotes

Origen—most distinguished and influential writer of the ancient church except possibly Augustine; used 18,000 New Testament quotations

Eusebius—"the Father of Church History" quoted the New Testament 5,000 times.

Jerome—translator of the Vulgate (see below)

Augustine

Note that we have an unbroken line of contact from the first to the third century. Jesus taught John who taught Polycarp who taught Irenaeus.

The sum of the discussion up to this point is this: we have available to scholars today sufficient evidence to determine with a high degree of accuracy what the text of the original manuscripts was. Careful translations will put in our hands, then, the Word of God which He intended us to have from the beginning.

II. Early History of the English Bible.

There are numerous versions to be encountered in a study of the history of the Bible, but we will mention but a few.

A. Septuagint. The Septuagint is the Greek translation of the Hebrew Old Testament. The work took place over about 100 years, 250-150 B.C., and it was the labor of Alexandrian Jews. Hebrew had been replaced, practically speaking, by Aramaic and then by Greek, so a Greek translation was needed by the people. It included the 39 books of the Old Testament plus the apocryphal books, though they were never included in the Hebrew Bible. The Septuagint is important for several reasons:

1. It is the first and oldest of Bible translations.
2. It is the Bible quoted extensively by Christ and the New Testament writers.
3. It was the Bible of the Early Church.
4. It is the basis for many later translations.

B. Vulgate. The Latin Vulgate is of great importance. The name means "common" or "current." It was translated by Jerome about A.D. 383-405. As far as the Old Testament is concerned, Jerome's source was the Septuagint. He was a well-qualified scholar, knowing Greek, Hebrew, and Latin. At the Council of Trent (1545-63) his translation was named "Vulgate" and declared the standard and authoritative Bible of the Roman Church.

Other versions followed through history as need demanded: the Coptic (Egyptian), as early as A.D. 250; the Georgian (part of Russia today), A.D. 330; Armenian, A.D. 436; Gothic, fifth or sixth century; Slavonic, ninth century or later; and Arabic.

The Bible used in England prior to the Reformation was the Latin Vulgate—of little use to the ordinary person who did not know Latin and could not afford a copy of his own, anyway.

C. Early English translations. The earliest English translations of the Bible came into existence at about the same time that the printing press was invented in Holland. This invention took place in A.D. 1450, and up to the turn of that century, 14 languages were represented with printed translations of the Bible.

Miller lists 10 early translators who translated or paraphrased portions of the Bible into Old English or Anglo-Saxon or in Middle English, all of which preceded our modern English, which dates from about 1500. These 10 are: Caedmon (his work, by the way, was not a translation, but a poetic paraphrase; Caedmon could not read, but listening to the Scriptures read in Latin, he would paraphrase them poetically and beautifully); Aldehelm, Egbert, Bede, Alfred, Aldred, Aelfrick, Orm, Shoreham, and Rolle. Miller comments: "These [last] two versions are often combined and mentioned as the Shoreham-Rolle versions, representing South and North England. They had a wide circulation, and they created in the hearts of the people a hunger for larger portions of the Word of God, and prepared the way for Wycliffe's version of the complete Bible." (H. S. Miller: *General Biblical Introduction*, pp. 319, 322)

D. Wycliffe. To today's Christian, the name Wycliffe is well known. He is aware of the worldwide Bible translation work being carried on by the organization known widely as Wycliffe. This fine missionary enterprise takes its name from the man who gave us the first complete translation of the Bible in the English language. Prior to this time, the English versions had been only in pieces and parts.

Wycliffe lived and studied in a time of transition. The fourteenth century was a transitional period between the Middle Ages and the Reformation. Because of his outstanding work, Wycliffe came to be known as "The Morning Star of the Reformation" and "the first Protestant" (*Ibid.,* p. 325). His efforts were directed toward two aspects of one main purpose—making the Bible known to the masses. This was to be accomplished through the translation of the Bible and its transmission. Kenyon comments on these points as follows:

> His championship of the common people led him to undertake a work which entitles him to honourable mention by men of all parties and all opinions—the preparation of an English Bible which every man who knew his letters might read in his own home. And that even those who could not read, might receive the knowledge of the teachings of this Bible, he instituted his order of "poor priests" to go about and preach to the poor in their own tongue.

(Frederic G. Kenyon: *Our Bible and the Ancient Manuscripts,* p. 200)

Because of his great influence over the common people and his determination to stand against Romanism, Wycliffe was characterized by his enemies as "the organ of the devil, the enemy of the Church . . . the confusion of the common people . . . the son of the old Serpent, the forerunner of the Antichrist, who had completed his iniquity by inventing a new translation of the Scriptures" (Miller, *op. cit.,* p. 239).

His death came as a result of a sudden paralysis which his enemies explained as an act of the judgment of God.

The Wycliffe Bible was the only English Bible for 145 years and widespread was its influence. Still today our Bibles are tinged with the influence of Wycliffe. Such expressions as "the strait gate," "the narrow way," "the mote," and "the beam" have come down to us from his translation.

III. Versions Leading to the King James

Two events of the mid-fifteenth century exerted untold influence on Bible translation: the appearance of the first known product of the printing press in Europe (November 1454), and the fall of the Eastern Empire that drove to the West multitudes of able scholars who revived a zeal for the study of Hebrew and Greek and a consequent study of the Scriptures.

It is interesting to note that while the Bible existed in national languages in France, Spain, Italy, Bohemia, and Holland, and in Germany the Scriptures were printed in 1466, yet the Bible was not printed in English before 1525, and no complete Bible was printed in England before 1538.

A. Tyndale. Some regard the history of the English Bible to begin with Tyndale. His was the first printed edition of the Bible in English and is the prototype of the King James Version. Also, his is not a translation of a translation as was Wycliffe's (from the Vulgate), but a translation of the original Greek and Hebrew.

William Tyndale lived and studied during the beginning years of the Reformation. A conversation while he was a student reveals his purpose in life. Someone said to him, "We were better without God's law than without the Pope's," to which Tyndale replied, "I defy the Pope and all his laws; if God spares my life, ere many years I will cause a boy that driveth the plough shall know more of the Scripture than thou doest." (Miller, *op. cit.,* p. 334)

Tyndale suffered from what might be called a "fatal devotion" to the task of translation. He completed translating the

New Testament in Germany in 1525, and these first printed portions of the Bible in English were smuggled into England, which was overwhelmingly Catholic at that time. His action amounted to heresy and aroused violent persecution. The Inquisition finally caught him, and he was imprisoned, strangled, and burned at the stake in 1536.

His work was not in vain, though. The King James Version is "practically a fifth revision of Tyndale's, and it retains many of the words and much of the character, form, and style of his version," according to Kenyon (Frederic G. Kenyon: *The Story of Our Bible,* pp. 48-49).

B. Others. Many translations followed Tyndale's, but only a few are worthy of mention in this quick survey. One was known as the Coverdale Bible, published in 1535 by Miles Coverdale who had the prime minister Thomas Cromwell as his patron. His work was published with royal approval, incorporating most of Tyndale's best work.

The most popular Bible in England for private reading until 30 years after the publishing of the King James Version was the Geneva Bible. This translation was the work of a group of reformers that included John Calvin and John Knox; the New Testament was largely the work of William Whittingham. It went through 150 editions between 1560-64, and it included strong Calvinistic notes, chapters divided into verses, and italics to indicate words not in the original manuscripts. This is the Bible that was brought to the New World by the Pilgrims, who regarded it as their constitution.

All of these translations—and many more—were the work of Protestants. The Roman Church was slow to see the need for the Bible in the language of the common people because it had always insisted that it held greater authority than the Word of God and was actually the final authority in all things spiritual and moral. However, it finally did begin to prepare its own approved versions "for the more speedy abolishing . . . of false and impious translations put forth by sundry sectes" (preface of the Rheims New Testament quoted by the *Encyclopedia Britannica*).

C. King James Version. We come now to what is un-doubtedly the most common version of the English Bible in use yet today. It is recognized as a great literary work even by those who hold very low views of the inspiration of the Scriptures. Most of the Biblical terminology which is used in everyday expression is the terminology which comes from this version of the Bible.

This great work of translation was brought about by a genuine need for an accepted single version of the Bible and by the pride of a newly crowned king. The Geneva Bible was the favorite of the people and many of the clergy, but was not approved by the king or the religious hierarchy. King James VI of Scotland ascended the throne of England as King James I in 1603, and he authorized a new translation of the Scriptures, thinking primarily, no doubt, of the fame and prestige it would bring to him. It is said that 15 rules were set up for the translators to observe in their work; Robinson lists these five as the most important:

1) that they should follow the Bishops' Bible and alter as little as the truth of the originals would permit; 2) that no mar-ginal notes should be affixed except explanations of Hebrew and Greek words; 3) that the work should be done first individually and separately, and then reviewed by all the members of each company meeting together in conference; 4) that special diffi-culties should be submitted, if deemed necessary, to specialists outside their own number; and 5) that Tyndale's, Matthew's, Coverdale's, the Great Bible, and the Genevan versions should be used when they agree better with the original than the Bishops.

(George L. Robinson: *Where Did We Get Our Bible?*, p. 165)

Fifty-four scholars were appointed to do the work of trans-lation. Unique in this new version of the Scriptures was the inclusion of marginal references. This was undoubtedly the most carefully planned and executed English translation of the Bible at that time. The result was an excellent work, recognized as such by scholars of all faiths. "Even a Roman Catholic divine, Dr. Geddes (1786), declares that 'if accuracy and strictest attention to the letter of the text be supposed to constitute an excellent version, this is of all versions, the most excellent.'" (J. Patterson Smyth: *How We Got Our Bible*, p. 121)

Like almost all other attempts at a new translation, the King James Version did not immediately meet with wide acceptance. It was even bitterly attacked by some; but, nevertheless, by the end of the seventeenth century it was *the* Bible. Even today, some Bible-loving Christians, who may be untrained in textual history and problems, and so on, accept the Authorized Version as if it were the originally inspired Word of God.

There are some outstanding merits which might be noted in regard to this version. It was the work of not just one, but many scholars—which enables it to be more or less free of bias in interpretation. It was prepared with reference to the best English versions of the day and, more importantly, with reference to the original languages so that it was not a secondary translation. It is accepted, for the most part, as an accurate translation in light of the sources with which the work could be done. Its vocabulary and style are masterful, so that it has taken its place as a great scholarly work in English literature.

The major fault with this translation cannot properly be laid at the feet of the revision committee. They had a defective text to translate from. Subsequent discoveries of earlier manuscripts than were available to them have brought about other versions and revisions about which we speak later.

As testimony to the acceptance of the King James Version by the common people, hear this tribute by Willard L. Sperry, long dean of the Harvard Divinity School:

The King James Bible has been the one thread, above all others, on which the experience of the English-speaking people has been strung for over 300 years. ... But the scholar ... does not always realize to the full the measure to which Bible-reading Christians identify their experience not merely with the subject matter, but with the actual wording of the Authorized version.

The very words, in their familiar form, are something more than translation.

(Chamberlain and Felder: *The Dartmouth Bible*, p. xxxvi)

6

Bible Versions
and Translations

I. Reasons for Translations
   A. Better sources
   B. Language changes

II. Evaluation
   A. The translator's role
   B. Qualities
   C. Observations
   D. Paraphrases and translations
   E. Guidelines

III. Common Versions
   A. Recent versions
   B. Modern-speech versions

Which Bible should we use? Should we read the Living Bible, preach from the King James, and use the New American Standard in our study? With the multitude of versions and translations available today, the Bible-lover is faced with the task of choosing which one to use—or when to use which one. It would seem advisable to know something about the various Bibles available and how to evaluate and use them.

I. Reasons for Translations

After all, except for the Hebrew and Greek scholars, we are all dependent upon translations. Most of us cannot handle the Greek New Testament sufficiently well to carry it to church or Sunday School with us. All the Bible-reading and study of most Christians is from translations, revisions, or paraphrases. Opinions differ widely on the various versions, too. Because one is new does not mean it is good; the newest is not necessarily the best. Contrariwise, because it's new doesn't mean it's bad. F. F. Bruce comments that, "a good translation of the Bible is almost bound to be greeted with hostility at first." Even the King James Version was met with hatred and opposition at its first appearance. It was not completely accepted for some 200 years, in fact.

Why did we need new translations in the first place? Well, let's start with the King James Authorized Version of 1611. Why did it need replacing, if it did? It remained practically unchanged for 200 years. In fact, some English religious leaders were asserting that it was the true revelation of God, free from error in either thought or expression. But, that was not a universal opinion. There were several reasons why a revision was thought necessary in the late nineteenth century. Meanings of words in the KJV had changed; more ancient manuscripts had been discovered than were available to the translators of the early seventeenth century; methods of Biblical criticism had been developed to a higher efficiency; and there was a better knowledge of Hebrew and Greek.

A. Better sources. Today's editions of the Greek New Testament are far more accurate than those which were available in the sixteenth and seventeenth centuries. How greatly the situation has improved since then! We are getting closer and closer to the autographs of the New Testament, so that a modern translation of the Greek New Testament, strange as it may seem, is in fact a much older New Testament than the 1611 translation. (Robert G. Bratcher: "Why Do We Need New Translations?" in *Bible Versions and Bible Enjoyment,* pp. 25-26)

While there is always resistance to change, Wayne Kemp points out the fallacy of clinging to the old just because it has been so highly revered. "To persist in using an antiquated language has two effects. The KJV will become more *holy* and less *Bible* with a holy language. Secondly, God's original intention that the Scriptures be conveyed in the common language of the people will be destroyed." (Wayne Kemp: *Conservative Baptist Magazine,* Spring 1977)

B. Language changes. It can hardly be argued today that the language of the KJV is the language of the common people in the United States. True, it is English, but so is the work of Shakespeare, and many Americans struggle in understanding his magnificent plays. Note the following listing of a few of the hundreds of KJV terms that make this version hard to understand today:

"I do you to wit" means "I make known to you."

"All appearance of evil" doesn't mean "everything that looks as if it might be wrong," but "every form of evil."

"Let" doesn't mean "allow," but "hinder."

"Charity" doesn't mean "gifts for the poor"; it means "love."

"A publican sitting at the receipt of custom" is "a tax collector on a stool at the tax office."

"Sore" doesn't mean "painful"; it means "very much."

"Conversation" isn't "talk"; it means "manner of life."

"Bottles" are really "wineskins."

"Prayed" needn't mean "spoke to God"; it can mean, simply, "asked."

"Withered" means "paralyzed."

A "husbandman" is a "farmer."

"Forwardness" means "readiness."

"Frustrate" doesn't mean "annoy"; it means "make void."

(Henry Jacobsen: "Power for Living")

II. Evaluation

Not everyone, of course, would be able to evaluate a translation of the Biblical languages; we have to leave that to the scholars. But we can know something of the translator's responsibility and make judgments concerning his purpose and achievement.

A. The translator's role. As Dr. Bruce puts it:

A translator of the Bible has a twofold task. In view of the variety of readings exhibited by the manuscripts and versions at his disposal, he must repeatedly make up his mind which reading he is to adopt as the basis for his translation; and only then can he proceed with his task of translation. He must, in fact, be not only translator but something of a textual critic as well. (F. F. Bruce in *Christianity Today*, March 13, 1961)

The art of translation is a fascinating one. It is both a science and an art: a science, in that definite rules of language and meaning can be formulated and applied; art, because the process of communication involves the living element, beyond analysis and classification, which determines the meaning of the text. What the translator does is to grasp the meaning of the whole sentence, or paragraph, and then in the appropriate idiom and usage of the language in which he is translating, give the equivalent meaning, approximately, as much as the genius of his language allows, the vocabulary and the style of the original. (Bratcher, *op. cit.*, p. 26)

A caution might be raised in considering Bible versions. One can make certain judgments by observing a few things about the translators. Is the version in question the work of a single translator or a team of scholars? The greater the number of scholars from varied backgrounds, the greater the chance of a work that is not "slanted" or biased. Since translators have to make theological decisions in their work, their theological bias should be considered. Ability and theology are two important factors to weigh. Conservative evangelicals are not likely to accept uncritically the translation work of liberal scholars no matter how qualified their academics, nor the work of fundamentalists who lack sufficient training, no matter how orthodox their faith.

B. Qualities. There are certain qualities that one must look for in any worthy translation of the Bible. The first is *accuracy*. The question is not, "Is the idea expressed attractively?" but "Does it render faithfully the thought of the original?" As to accuracy, Henry Jacobsen put it this way: "The difference between the right word and the nearly right word is the difference between a lightning bolt and a lightning bug." A second quality is *clarity*. Is the translation clear, understandable? Why a new translation—if it confuses or fails to clarify? A third consideration—not essential, but important—is *style*. The text should be smooth and easy, a pleasure to read. One of the virtues of the KJV is its elegance. Style is important, and different readers will appreciate different styles, choosing the one that suits them. That's fine, as long as the accuracy and clarity are not sacrificed for style. The Bible should be easy to read and understand, and enjoyable, too. But first, it must be accurate!

Another consideration in evaluation is the audience for whom a version may be prepared. If a translation is prepared for a particular religious group, you must be aware of the probability of theological bias. Of some translation attempts one might well ask, "What was the purpose the translators had in mind?" "What were they trying to prove?" The purpose ought to be to render the original languages into as accurate and clear and readable a translation as possible—not to prove something.

C. Observations. Finally, regarding translations, here are some observations that might be of help:

1. There is no such thing as a "totally accurate" translation. There is no such thing as a word-for-word translation. Word order cannot easily be duplicated in a translation.
2. A certain tension exists between the desire to make a transla-

tion modern and understandable and the necessity to keep in the reader's mind the fact that he is handling a piece of ancient literature which requires, for its proper understanding, an ancient setting.

3. Christian theology must never rest on the shaky foundation of being one language removed from the original. For maximum accuracy, revealed truth must be studied in the original languages.

(Robert H. Mounce: "How to Evaluate New Bible Versions" in *Bible Versions and Bible Enjoyment*, pp. 27-28)

D. Paraphrases and translations. A comment ought to be made about paraphrases as contrasted with translations. One of the most popular Bibles today is *The Living Bible,* which puts the Scriptures into modern "newspaper style" English, very easy to read and understand. It is a paraphrase. A paraphrase differs drastically from a translation. The former attempts to word a translation in more understandable language; it is the rendering of one sentence into another, trying to say the same thing in different words. Usually the thought is considered of primary importance with little attention given to exact words and word order.

Paraphrases are useful, but there are dangers in their use, too. One danger is that the words of Scripture lose their authority. Without attention to which Greek or Hebrew word is used in a text, it is difficult to base theology on a paraphrase of that text. Another danger relates to the misuse of a paraphrase. The reader may try to base theological perspective and decisions on his reading and may misunderstand. In contrast, a translation is another matter. The translator faithfully renders the original text into another language in the most accurate fashion possible. Word order and word choice are of importance; he is interested in the sense of a passage, of course, but also in the exact wording.

E. Guidelines. In using various versions of the Bible, the careful Bible student will want to keep a few guidelines in mind. As suggested above, he will want to know something of the translator(s) and the purpose for the version he's using, the audience for which it's intended, any theological bias which might be expected, and so on. Then, too, his own purpose in using the text is significant. Is it purely for devotional reading? If so, he may use a version which reads easily and at the same time has a style which elevates and exalts. If for study, he will want to use the most accurate version he can find, one that carefully conveys the word choices and word order most closely reflecting the originals. He will want to choose the work of respected scholars whose theological qualifications are unquestioned.

On the other hand, if one is choosing a text to use in personal witnessing or counseling with the unsaved or immature Christian, he will likely want to use a paraphrase—something that is easily read and understood, that does not require a prior acquaintance with and mastery of theological or Biblical terminology. Like pablum and baby food, he may want to begin with what is more easily digested and then move to the more "meaty" things after a little growth and appetite is developed.

For the individual who is acquainted with the original languages of the Scriptures, it ought to be obvious that he should use the Hebrew Bible and his Greek New Testament to determine what is the proper rendering of the text. In public use, such as the pulpit or classroom, it would seem advisable to use the version which is commonly used by the audience; today, that may be either the King James Version or the New American Standard Bible (discussed later). The careful student, of course, will consult other versions in his studies; many will be helpful for reference.

It may sound strange to admit it, but while the great number of available versions of the Bible today may bring some confusion, there is some value in a multiplicity of texts, too.

If one will equip himself with several of the translations and compare them from time to time in his reading, he will be impressed with their basic agreement. The measure of disagreement may prove to be a blessing in disguise. It may provoke the reader to new thoughts as new shades of meaning are suggested for passages which long since have ceased to stimulate inquiry because they are so familiar. (Everett F. Harrison: "The Bible in Your Language," *Youth for Christ Magazine*, February 1972)

III. Common Versions

To list all the versions, revisions, translations, and paraphrases which are available to the reader would be impossible here. We shall list only a few, with brief descriptions or comments in just two groups: recent versions, complete translations of teams of scholars that are widely accepted; and modern-speech versions, often the work of a single translator.

A. Recent versions.

1. English Revised—chiefly the responsibility of the Church of England whose purpose was to replace the KJV with a more up-to-date work. Largely a revision of the KJV, it appeared in segments in 1881, 1885, and 1895. It is worthy of note that while the purpose of the English committee was to provide a Bible for the common people, its chief use today is by scholars, and it is anything but popular with the common people.

2. American Standard Version—this is a recension of the English edition just discussed. Published in 1901, it continues, completes, and in many instances corrects the work of the earlier version. This text was widely accepted and was used in scholarly circles where a more accurate Bible for study purposes was desired. To some degree, it has been replaced now by the New American Standard Bible (see next page).

3. Revised Standard Version—finally completed in 1952, this was an attempt to make the preceding versions more readable, since they tended to be more scholarly. This translation has not been very well received in conservative circles. It has been circulated extensively among the laymen and clergy of "religious" America, since it is the product of the National Council of Churches; but it has been objectionable to many who see it as having a liberal theological bias.

4. New World Translation—the Jehovah's Witnesses published their version of the Bible in 1950. It is regarded as a more or less faithful rendering into vernacular English; but its notes, of course, are highly prejudiced to the publisher's theological viewpoint and concepts. It is included in this listing only to alert the reader to the fact that not every modern version of the Bible—however scholarly—is the product of orthodox Christianity.

5. New English Bible—an attempt on the part of a large and representative team of scholars from Great Britain and Ireland to produce a completely new translation from the original languages into the English of today. This version appeared in the '60s and has been issued in various portions under different titles. The New Testament has been distributed widely in an edition called "Good News for Modern Man." It has been criticized by conservatives for the omission of the word "blood" from 15 New Testament texts and similar omissions that seem to suggest theological bias in several important doctrinal areas.

6. New American Standard Bible—the successor to the American Standard Version of 1901, this newer translation has found the widest reception of any modern translation among conservative Christians. The New Testament was published as early as 1960, and the entire Bible appeared later. The Lockman Foundation, publishers, expressed a fourfold aim: "1) these publications shall be true to the original Hebrew and Greek; 2) they shall be grammatically correct; 3) they shall be understandable to the masses; 4) they shall give the Lord Jesus Christ His proper place, the place which the Word gives Him; no work will ever be personalized." In this writer's opinion, at the present time, this is the most suitable and useful English Bible readily available.

7. New International Bible—purported to become the most widely acceptable to Bible-lovers is this newly completed version. The New Testament has been available for

a few years already. It is the work of a whole host of scholars from around the world who are working in committees to prepare fresh translations from the original languages; thus, it is not a rehash or revision of someone else's work. It is in an easy reading style and is understandable to the average person. Some have expressed the hope that this will finally be the version to supplant the KJV in the minds and hearts of Christians everywhere, so that the confusion caused by the mass of different translations will be put to an end. Only time will tell!

B. Modern-speech versions.

1. Weymouth Testament—published in 1903, this work of Dr. R. F. Weymouth of England is "an idiomatic translation into everyday English from the text of the resultant Greek Testament." Regarded highly, it is especially fine in its sensitivity to the shades of meaning conveyed by the various tenses of the Greek verb. It is simple, but dignified.

2. Moffatt Testament—James Moffatt produced his second Testament in 1913; it is considered a "strikingly independent" modern-speech work. Harrison calls it "brilliantly done" but suggests it is marred because the translator occasionally followed inferior manuscript authority.

3. Williams' Testament—produced in 1937 and called "A Translation in the Language of the People," Williams, in this version, paid strict attention to the exact shades of meaning of the Greek tenses—sometimes "over-translating" in the opinion of some. On the other hand, others regard this work as "almost indispensable, of unusual excellence, worthy of rank among the very best."

4. Berkeley Version—the purpose of the translator, Gerrit Verkuyl, was to produce a "translation less interpretative than Moffatt's, more cultured in language than Goodspeed's, more American than Weymouth's, and freer from the King James than the Revised Standard."

5. Phillips' Translation—beginning with "Letters to Young Churches," in 1948, which was a rendering of the

Epistles, the entire New Testament was completed in 1958. The work is really an expansion on the text and a paraphrase rather than a literal translation.

6. Amplified Bible—the New Testament appeared in 1958 and the whole Bible in subsequent years. As its title suggests, it amplifies the text by means of elucidating expansions and paraphrases, giving several readings for a single word or term. Consequently, it is helpful for study purposes but difficult for reading, and very impractical for public reading. One does not know which of the suggested terms may be the most appropriate in a given context because there is no help offered in selecting; they all appear.

7. The Living Bible—what began as a father's attempt to put portions of the Bible into understandable English for his children at family devotions has developed into the most popular and best-selling Bible of our times. Kenneth Taylor has produced a free-flowing, easy-reading volume which is admittedly a paraphrase. As intended, it makes the Bible read like the daily newspaper, thus many who never read it before are reading the Bible with understanding.

The preceding list may be exhausting, though not exhaustive. These are probably the versions that most of our readers will come across in the normal circumstances of life, and if one exercises care in the purposes for which he uses them, many of them will be helpful to him.

Again, however, we emphasize that the Word of God was verbally inspired; that immediately suggests something about the importance of each word in the original. That translation will be most helpful, it would seem to this writer, then, that would most closely and accurately convey those original words into a style nearest to the language the reader understands most fully.

7

How To Use the Bible

It's good to have an appreciation for the Bible—what it is, how God gave it, how we got it, how reliable it is, and so forth—all of that is fine. But, the unopened Bible is of no value to anyone. It is not a work of art to be stared at nor a work of genius to be admired only at a distance. It is the most practical book in the world—but not if it's ignored!

There are many purposes for which one may open the Bible for reading or studying, and the purpose may well determine the manner in which he studies or the way in which he uses the Bible. In the next chapter, we will lay down certain guidelines and rules for interpreting Scripture; and those guidelines might be previewed at this point with some profit. Our purpose here is to make some suggestions as to how one might use the Bible with both personal benefit and a ministry to others.

I. Devotional Use

It has often been said that a Christian—be he preacher, teacher, or lay person—can minister to someone else only what is the overflow of his own heart. In other words, while you might be able to study for certain situations—sermons, classes, programs, and so on—your most effective ministry comes from what you've personally experienced and profited from. So, we begin our discussion with the use of the Bible for one's own personal and private devotional life. While that includes study, of course, we'll reserve the matter of studying the Bible for later in the chapter.

A. Benefits of Bible reading. There are numerous benefits to be expected from the reading of the Bible, when one is reading with understanding and with a willingness to respond in faith and obedience.

First of all, the Bible will alert the reader to sin; it will convict him of his sin. The Bible not only states what sin is, but it judges our motives, for it is sharp and it is a "discerner of the thoughts and intents of the heart" (Heb. 4:12). It is a mirror which reflects our lives and conduct and makes judgments about them (see James 1:23-24); it was given for the purpose of reproof and correction (see II Tim. 3:16). So, perusing the Scriptures will convict of sin.

Furthermore, the reading of the Bible can bring cleansing from the pollution of sin. David testified that it was God's Word that cleansed the way of the young man (see Ps. 119:9). Paul says that we may be cleansed by "the washing of water by the word" (Eph. 5:26). How wonderful that the Bible not only convicts us of sin, but cleanses us as well! As the believer reads the Word and is made aware of his sin, he is able to acknowledge that sin before God and receive the cleansing which is promised (see I John 1:9).

The Bible imparts strength to the faithful reader. Peter exhorts us to feed upon the Word like a baby does upon milk "that ye may grow thereby" (I Peter 2:2). The writer of Hebrews refers to the Christian's feeding on the meatier, heavier things of spiritual truth. These bring growth and maturity (see Heb. 5:12, 14). Job stated that the words of God were more precious to him than food (see Job 23:12). Surely, every Christian could testify to the personal strength he has received as he has read the Bible prior to, or in the midst of, times of special strain or trial.

The Bible also gives instruction as to what the Christian is to do. It is our guidebook, our manual of procedure, our road map through "pilgrim's progress." Again, this is one of its purposes; it is "profitable . . . for instruction in righteousness" (II Tim. 3:16). It is not something only to be read or heard for appreciation; it is something to respond to, something to do. James warns of the dangers in hearing without doing—we are to be doers, not hearers only (see James 1:22). The Christian need never lack for something to do; he need not seek unsuccessfully for instruction or direction. He need only consult the Scriptures; the game plan is spelled out for him in detail. Where he lacks wisdom about specifics in his own life and circumstance, he still has sufficient instruction for shaping and directing his life.

The Bible is the believer's source of strength and, at the

same time, his chief tool or weapon against sin. We are admonished to use shield and armor for our protection and to take the "sword of the Spirit" which is identified as "the word of God" (see Eph. 6:17). With it we fight off Satan and temptation; with it we bolster our confidence and strength; with it we conquer for Christ in gaining spiritual growth and in producing spiritual fruit.

Psalm 1 illustrates that the Bible makes our lives fruitful. As we meditate in the "law" (the Word of God), we are like the planted tree that produces fruit. Apart from the Word, there is no fruit, for apart from the Word, our relationship with God deteriorates and becomes unproductive.

At some length, then, we have enumerated the benefits of Bible reading. How does one go about it? Is there some formula for Bible reading that will guarantee instant success: "Ten days of Bible reading and you'll be able to live victoriously, have all you want, never be depressed, etc., etc."? Beware of easy formulas. While we can learn a lot from the experience of successful Christians and their Bible reading habits, what we suggest here are merely guidelines to make your reading more helpful and useful.

B. Preparing for Bible reading. Helpful Bible reading undoubtedly begins with prayer. The Holy Spirit is the author of the Scriptures. He "moved along" the holy men who recorded God's revelation (see II Peter 1:21). He's the one who Jesus promised would guide us into all truth and teach us all things (see John 14:26; 16:13). Keeping in mind that the Bible is a divine book, the reader can ask its author and primary teacher to illuminate his mind as he reads the book. A simple, sincere prayer that God will make His Word meaningful and practical as it is read is the starting point for profitable Bible reading.

C. Suggestions for Bible reading. It sounds oversimplified, to be sure, but one writer has suggested that we read slowly. That's more important than it may seem at first. Read slowly. Speed-reading courses are not of great value to the person who wants to feed upon the Word of God. He must savor the words as bites of tasty nourishment; he must linger at the refreshing pools of divine counsel and wisdom. He must not confuse the number of verses or chapters read with the achieving of growth or health.

Systematic reading is important, too. The Bible is referred to sometimes as "the whole counsel of God." Do we ignore parts of that counsel in our reading? Do we read just those passages which are familiar or poetically beautiful? Do we avoid the difficult, the unpleasant, the "too close to home" portions? Whether you determine to read the whole Bible through in a given period of time, or choose to skip from Old to New Testaments, or follow some other scheme, be sure to read it all. And the only way to be sure is to have some plan or system.

In devotional reading, make yours a very personal matter; read for your own need; find its applications for you. You're not reading now in order to prepare a lesson for some class or to gain help to offer a counselee; you're reading to know God, to grow in grace; so, keep the reading personal.

Two other suggestions that have been stated before or will be mentioned later in other connections, but which pertain to personal, devotional reading, too: keep in mind the context of what you're reading and put into practice what you're learning. Do not allow yourself to make personal applications that are completely out of keeping with the basic meaning of the passage. The humorous—to the point of ridiculous—illustration is "Judas went out and hanged himself. Go thou and do likewise." If you do not keep the context in mind, you may misapply Scripture in equally disastrous ways. But, do apply the Scriptures to your own life. Respond to what you're reading with faith to accept it and with a willingness to obey it. In that manner, your life will be strengthened and you will grow as you read.

D. Guidelines for Bible reading. Let's summarize those matters just discussed and add a few more to give a list of guidelines for your personal Bible reading. Remember, this is not a formula to guarantee anything, it is merely a list to consider if your Bible reading needs a boost.

1. Read carefully, like the Bereans of Acts 17:11.
2. Read trustfully—that is, with a willingness to believe; remember, without faith, it is impossible to please God (see Heb. 11:6).
3. Read enough to develop some continuity of thought; that may require a whole chapter, at least a paragraph in prose, perhaps only a verse or two in poetry.
4. Read consecutively; avoid complicated systems but follow some simple scheme which will guide you through the whole Bible.
5. Keep your mind on the subject; when your mind starts to wander, go back and repeat what you've read and follow suggestion No. 6.
6. Read aloud; it may surprise you what that will do to make the Bible more dramatic, to keep your mind on what you're doing, and to bring new words or ideas to your attention.
7. Read selfishly—not for a class or a friend, but for yourself.
8. Read with pen in hand; keep a diary of new ideas and personal applications; perhaps you can jot down subjects for study at a later time.

E. Meditation in Bible reading. Before we move to a consideration of study uses of the Bible, let's mention a very important word in regard to reading and studying the Bible: meditation. The psalmist wrote that the godly man delights in the law of the Lord "and in his law doth he meditate day and night" (Ps. 1:2). The Lord instructed Israel's new leader, the successor to Moses: "This book of the law shall not depart out of thy mouth? but thou shalt meditate therein day and night" (Joshua 1:8). While we may read a lot of the Bible and study a lot, how much meditating do we do? You have no doubt heard the description of meditation which likens it to the cow chewing her cud. With a multiple-stomach system, the cow swallows her food only to disgorge it at a later time to chew on it some more.

To get the maximum out of the Word of God, the reader must chew on it repeatedly and at length. Meditation is not just reading and understanding, it is reflecting. Irving Jensen suggests five aspects of this kind of reflection:

1. Reflect purposefully; this is not mind-wandering time, it's concentrated thinking in a limited area of revelation.
2. Reflect imaginatively; visualize the setting, put yourself in the text.
3. Reflect humbly; this is the Holy Revelation of God; don't limit it by merely thinking about what human wisdom says about it.
4. Reflect prayerfully: "Open thou mine eyes, that I may behold wondrous things out of thy law" (Ps. 119:18).
5. Reflect patiently: wait on the Lord!

(Irving L. Jensen: *Enjoy Your Bible,* pp. 34-39)

Andrew Murray pointed out that our intellect gathers and prepares the food; while in meditating, the heart takes it in and feeds upon it.

II. Study Use

Almost all of what has been said already is applicable when it comes to Bible study. We need to begin with the same kind of preparation and with the same attitude. Our approach is different only in that we are now giving ourselves to careful analysis of a given subject or in preparation for a given responsibility.

A. Guidelines for study. As above, we should begin with prayer, reading of the Bible, meditation, determination to obey what we discover and to pass it on to others. In this section, we will limit ourselves pretty much to the suggestion of methods of Bible study. The novice may want to begin with easy passages; start studying the more familiar Scriptures;

be willing to obey what he learns; and be especially sensitive to the Holy Spirit's teaching.

At the outset, the present writer would recommend a very excellent paperback book that any student would find helpful. It's entitled *Profitable Bible Study,* written by the late Wilbur M. Smith. One chapter presents eight methods of Bible study. That alone is worth the price of the book, but there's much more of value, too.

B. Methods of study. Perhaps the simplest method of Bible study may be called the *unit* method. That simply takes a single unit of the text and devotes its efforts to an analysis and understanding of that unit. The unit could be an entire book of the Bible, a single chapter, paragraph, or verse. As you study, ask yourself these questions:

1. What meaning did this have for the original readers?
2. What is the main subject of the unit?
3. How does the passage concern me?
4. Which is the best verse in this chapter (paragraph)?
5. Who are the principal persons involved?
6. What does the chapter (unit) teach concerning Christ?
7. Are there any examples for me to follow? any errors to avoid?
8. Are there any duties for me to perform? any promises to claim?
9. Are there any prayers for me to echo?

Now, these are simple enough, aren't they? And they do relate to personal, devotional study as much as to studious analysis. For the more studious analysis, keep in mind, also, the principles of interpretation which you will find in chapter 8.

In addition to the unit method of Bible study, there are others. You could make a *geographical* study, considering everything you can find in the Bible about Egypt, Jerusalem, the Holy Land, and so forth. Study the missionary journeys of Paul, the wanderings of Israel, the areas visited by Jesus.

Or, you could make *biographical* studies—the lives of Jesus, Paul, Moses, the 12 sons of Jacob, the apostles. The Bible is replete with rich biographical material.

Almost limitless are the *topical* studies you could pursue in the Bible. Take a great doctrine of the faith, a profession or vocation, miracles. In this category we could include *word* studies. Check the chapter on Bible study aids to find those particular tools you'll need for profitable word study, because a simple listing of the English words and their meanings may be misleading. However, word studies can be rich and fulfilling. After all, most of our expression in communication—at least what is recordable—is in words. We do not have any pictures of God or Jesus, but we have thousands of words that convey His revelation.

How about pursuing a study in which you'll attempt to *find Christ* in all the Scriptures? Can you find Him in the Gospels? Of course. The epistles? Surely. What about the law? Yes, He is the fulfillment of the law; but how? In the prophets and Psalms? In the Revelation? Much can be learned by such a study.

It is said of Martin Luther that he studied the Word the same way he gathered apples. First he shook the whole tree, that the ripest fruit might fall; afterward each limb, then each branch, next every twig, and finally he looked under every leaf. In other words, he began by reading the Bible as a whole, as he would any other volume. He then took time to shake every limb—studying the Scriptures more carefully, a book at a time. Next he would examine every branch and twig, giving attention to each chapter, paragraph, and sentence. At last he would look under each "leaf" by searching out the full meaning of the individual words. There are other methods of study, but Luther's certainly is a good one.

C. Making notes in study. Earlier we suggested that you keep a pen and paper handy when you're doing your devotional reading. Well, in Bible study, making notes is absolutely indispensable. What is not written is forgotten! That's an inexorable axiom that we've all come to appreciate, often too late, when we can't remember what we have already learned about something, and we have to study it all over again. So, make notes! As you're studying, write down these four things at least:

1. The main point of the passage (you may want to record sub-points for later study).

2. Cross references and what they add to the subject. Look them up and write down the significant content.

3. Problems and difficulties—for further study. Consult other students and writers on the passage/subject. Don't quit studying just because you haven't solved all the difficulties.

4. Applications. Find the primary meaning of the passage, but also list the appropriate applications. What is expected of you? What should we do?

III. Application

Bible study and devotional reading are of limited value if the truths we discover are not applied to life, and if they go without the proper response. In reading and studying, we should first look for personal applications. It's always easy to see how the Bible applies to other people, how they should change; but we should first look for the application to our personal life. Being a doer of the Word and not a hearer only describes the man who is making personal application. He is brought to worship the author of the book; he repents of the sin he's convicted about; he accepts what he learns in faith and is obedient to its precepts, witnessing in light of his learning.

After we have applied the Word to our own lives, it will be helpful to see its practical applications to others. We may be counseling with or witnessing to someone, and we find scriptural principles which directly bear on his/her need or situation. Our Bible study will be doubly rewarding if we are able to see those applications, lovingly share them, and cooperatively put them into practice. It is the privilege of the Christian to evangelize the lost—and the Word of God is applicable to that need; and to edify the saints—and we are equipped by the Word to so edify one another.

Jensen succinctly summarizes what we're trying to say in this chapter:

When you read the Bible, always be sure you are *really* reading it. Alert your eyes to see (Reading); stir up your mind to consider (Reflection); write down your observations (Recording); and practice what you read (Response). (*Ibid.*, p. 42)

8

On Interpreting the Bible

"You can prove anything from the Bible." Have you ever heard that kind of statement? Probably you have, and there's an element of truth in it, too. Not that the Bible is inconsistent and contradictory at all—we tried to establish in chapter 2 that it is a harmonious unit—but if one takes portions or statements out of their context, or twists and misapplies a particular text of Scripture, he can "prove" just about anything. There are certain basic rules and procedures to follow in correctly interpreting literature of any kind, especially the Bible, and it's those rules we want to discuss in this chapter.

Do you remember sitting in literature classes in school and having the teacher ask, "What did Shakespeare (or Burns or Shelley or Milton) mean when he wrote . . . . ?" My sophomoric reaction always was, "Well, he said what he meant; and if that isn't what he meant, why did he say it?" I was unwilling to dig into the texts to determine the symbolic, hidden, or deeper meanings of the author. Perhaps that's why literature was little more than an enjoyable pastime to me in those days. We cannot approach great literature with that attitude if we are to gain anything from it. Far more important, however, is the attitude with which we approach the study of the Scriptures!

The guiding text for the Bible student is "Study to shew thyself approved unto God, a workman that needeth not to be ashamed, rightly dividing the word of truth" (II Tim. 2:15). It's the "dividing" of the truth or "handling accurately the word of truth" (NASB) that this chapter is concerned with. The first hint for Bible interpretation is in the word "study." One does not casually read the Bible with any expectation of understanding its depths. The primary principle in interpretation must be *study*. We hope to show here some guidelines for the kind of study that enables one to rightly divide the truth.

I. Basic Principles

In chapter 7 we had something to say regarding the study of the Bible for personal and devotional use; and in chapter 9 we'll discuss certain aids for that study. Here, our purpose is to establish some principles for interpreting the Bible. How do we know, specifically and finally, what the Bible teaches on a particular doctrine or Christian principle? How do we come to understand the difficult portions of the Word? As suggested above, it all begins with the attitude we bring to our study.

A. Spiritual attitude. Scriptural truths are spiritually understood. Divine illumination of the Holy Spirit is the key that opens the meaning of Scripture. Paul writes about " . . . comparing spiritual things with spiritual. But the natural man receiveth not the things of the Spirit of God: for they are foolishness unto him: neither can he know them, because they are spiritually discerned" (I Cor. 2:13-14). The unconverted person does not receive Bible truth because the Holy Spirit, the one able to make the Bible plain, does not indwell the unsaved. We must be born into God's family if we expect to understand God's language. One's personal and momentary relationship with God is extremely important to his ability to understand and interpret Scripture.

B. Infallible rule. Having a right relationship with the author of the Scriptures and determining to search out the deep things of the Word, the student is now ready to apply certain rules or follow certain guidelines in his study. The first basic principle to follow is what is spoken of as "the infallible rule of interpretation." "The infallible rule of interpretation of Scripture is the Scripture itself; and therefore, when there is a question about the true and full sense of any scripture (which is not manifold but one), it must be searched and known by other places that speak more clearly." (Westminster Confession of Faith, Chapter I, Sec. ix)

That rule simply means to compare Scripture with Scripture. If you are considering the meaning of a particular word in the Bible, then search out the other uses of that word to find out what it means elsewhere. If it's a topic or subject, a historical event, or whatever, locate the other pertinent references in the Bible and get the light that they will add to your understanding. A concordance, listing all passages using the same word or term, will be invaluable in such a study, as will a topical index (see chapter 9). The infallible rule also suggests that you use the clear to interpret the more difficult. When one passage seems to have a simple and obvious meaning, it will be helpful in using that meaning to understand the more difficult passage where the meaning is more obscure.

C. Problems. Another basic principle to keep in mind is that times have changed between the writing of the books of the Bible and today. That's obvious, isn't it? Yet some try to make the Bible say things in the twentieth century that are completely outside of any reasonable interpretation when you consider the time and setting in which it was written. Keep in mind several problems involved in the right understanding of Scripture.

1. The English language has changed. If you're using a King James Version, keep in mind that in 1611 many words had entirely different definitions than they have today. The obvious illustration is I Thessalonians 4:15 where the word "prevent" in the KJV means to "precede" or "go before," not to "stop" or "hinder," as it does today. (More about these problems back in chapter 6.)

2. Remember, too, that customs have changed. We don't generally offer water at the door for our house guests to wash their feet when they come for a visit, but they did in Bible times. Now, we offer a friendly handshake (not usually even a Biblical "holy kiss"), and we suggest they can use the washroom, if they wish, before dinner. An understanding of Biblical customs will aid greatly in interpreting and applying the Scripture.

3. There are difficult passages. No one can ever truthfully say, "I understand the Bible completely." If it is the Word of God, as indeed it is, it will not be so easily understood by human minds. Isaiah quoted God as saying: "For my thoughts are not your thoughts, neither are your ways my

ways, saith the Lord. For as the heavens are higher than the earth, so are my ways higher than your ways, and my thoughts than your thoughts" (Isa. 55:8-9). Peter confessed that there "are some things hard to be understood" (II Peter 3:16). We cannot expect to get full understanding of everything, nor to learn it all at once. We should learn progressively as we give ourselves to diligent study.

4. There are differing settings. Some of these ideas will be expressed below, but, as you study the Bible, try to keep in mind the setting of the passage you're looking at. What is the place from which it's written? The place where it's being first sent? Who is writing? To whom? Why is it being written; what is its primary purpose? During what period of time did it appear? What meaning did it have for its first readers? Answers to these questions will greatly aid your understanding of the passage's significance for you today.

II. Forms of Expression

We must quickly note various forms of expression used in the Bible. As indicated elsewhere, some of the Bible is poetry and other is prose. Some is prophetic (foretelling) and other is historical narrative. Our understanding will come much more readily when we recognize the form of expression being used in the passage we're examining.

A. Forms. Wesley Walters suggests several helpful ideas in this connection:

Discover the form of expression. Is it literal or figurative? If figurative, ask: what *point* is being made? What *idea* is being expressed?

1. Words and phrases may be figurative: "my cup runneth over" or "blood that speaketh."

2. Actions and objects may bear figurative sense, such as a TYPE—it looks forward to a spiritual reality (the sacrificial lamb, for example). SYMBOL—it looks to present or past reality (the Lord's Supper).

3. Narratives may have a figurative meaning, as: ALLEGORY—an actual historic event which teaches a spiritual truth (Gala-

tians 4:2ff). PARABLE—a possible but not necessarily actual happening used as illustration (Christ taught by many parables). FABLE—an imaginary event beyond possibility of happening, used as illustration (Judges 9:6ff).

In dealing with figurative material remember: concentrate on the main point. Don't try to prove *too much* from it. Base your teaching on direct statements. Use the figurative mainly as illustrations. Notice in your Bible reading how the New Testament your guide. (Wesley Walters: "How To Read and Understand the Bible," pp. 10-12)

B. Typology. A further comment about typology seems in order. A type is a double representation, the literal being intended and planned to represent the spiritual. A literal event, person, or thing is used to represent a spiritual truth. By the use of types in the Bible we are often able to understand great spiritual ideas through the illustration of those literal, material things or events. The story of Ruth, for example, is more than a mere love story; it illustrates the truth of redemption by the Kinsman-Redeemer. That does not discount the historicity of the account; it actually did happen as recorded. But, it also has a rich significance for the believer today.

I Corinthians 10:11 teaches that the events of the Old Testament occurred for our benefit. They are types or illustrations of valuable truth for us. By typology, God makes His Word relevant for every age and circumstance. The danger in studying types, however, is that one might try to make every historical event or person a type of some spiritual truth while, in reality, it may not be at all. The safest procedure to follow is to see types where the Bible clearly uses them (comparing Scripture with Scripture) and avoid the temptation to make everything a type of some spiritual truth.

III. Rules of Interpretation

Before we list a number of helpful guidelines in interpretation, let us emphasize an important consideration that we've not mentioned before. That is that Scripture is not subject to many interpretations. We don't mean that there aren't many interpretations being suggested by students of the Word, but that there is but one correct interpretation of the Scriptures. Over the centuries, orthodox Christianity has had a great deal of unanimity in understanding the cardinal doctrines of the faith. Consult the great statements of faith over the years of church history, and you'll find that the Christian faith can be defined and described quite clearly.

It is the task of the student to interpret the Bible in a consistent and logical manner. He *may* find many *applications* of the various teachings of the Word—and rightly so, for the Bible is varied and diverse in its applications—but he *may not* find a variety of *interpretations* and pass them off as what the Scripture means. He must find a single, correct meaning. That's where the "rules" come in.

A. Three laws. Basic to the rules is the so-called "Golden Rule of Interpretation": "When the plain sense of Scripture makes common sense, seek no other sense; therefore, take every word at its primary, ordinary, usual, literal meaning, unless the facts of the immediate context, studied in the light of related passages and axiomatic and fundamental truths, indicate clearly otherwise." That's a far-reaching rule, isn't it? Following it would save many a misinterpretation. In fact, someone put it this way, "If one follows this rule, he will never go wrong; if he fails to follow it, he will never go right." The Golden Rule is so simple yet so comprehensive! Stick to it, and you'll be spared many fanciful and erroneous conclusions.

A second rule of interpretation is called the "Law of recurrence" which is: "that peculiarity of the Holy Spirit as an author in which He first states a fact in outline and then returns to it for the purpose of adding detail." For example, you have the creation of man in Genesis 1 mentioned as a simple statement of fact in the listing of the days of creation, but enlarged in the next chapter with some important detail.

A third rule is referred to as the "Law of double reference."

Many subjects in Scripture are discussed in more than one passage. By studying both—or all—references, you gain a complete picture which would be incomplete by noting just one. For example, both Ezekiel 20 and Isaiah 14 relate something of the fall of Satan from favor as an angel of God to become His adversary. Neither passage alone gives the full story. Be sure to look for additional references on any given subject you're studying in the Bible.

B. Nixon's rules. R. E. Nixon lists a number of rules on How to Understand the Bible" that you will find most helpful. They have been liberally rephrased in this writing:

1. The Biblical writers wrote *sense;* their words must be construed as to give a sensible meaning to them.
2. The meaning can be derived only from a consideration of the *whole* and every part of it.
3. The fundamental rule of interpretation to which all others are subordinate is that [the Bible] is to be expounded according to the intent of them that made it! This is the principle of "literal" interpretation which in its true sense means to discover the intention of the Biblical writer.
4. The purpose of the writer must be recognized in order to rightly understand its meaning.
5. Words are to be construed in their popular sense and in the sense they bore at the time of their writing.
6. The same words bear the same meaning unless the context clearly demands a change.

(R. E. Nixon: "Bible Versions and Bible Enjoyment," pp. 12-13. Nixon therein refers to "The Construction of Deeds and Statutes" by Sir Charles Odger and relates the principles for interpretation of statutes to Bible interpretation.)

C. Stott's sound principles. John R. W. Stott suggests these sound principles of interpretation:

1. We must look for the *natural* sense—the principle of simplicity—because we believe that God intended His revelation to be a plain and readily intelligible communication to ordinary human beings.
2. We must look for the *original* sense—the principle of history—because we believe that God addressed His Word to those who

first heard it, and that it can be received by subsequent generations only in so far as they understand it historically. Our
understanding may be fuller than that of the first hearers (e.g.
of the prophecies of Christ); it cannot be substantially different.
3. We must look for the *general* sense—the principle of harmony—
because we believe that God is self-consistent, and that His
revelation is self-consistent, too.

(John R. W. Stott: *Understanding the Bible,* pp. 217-238)

John Wycliffe's "Rules of Interpretation" will serve as a
suitable summary for this chapter:

It shall greatly help ye to understand Scripture,
If thou mark
Not only what is spoken or wrytten,
But of whom,
And to whom,
With what words,
At what time,
Where,
To what intent,
With what circumstances,
Considering what goeth before
And what followeth.

9

Helpful Aids for Bible Study

I. Study Bibles and Commentaries
   A. Bibles
   B. Commentaries

II. Reference Works
   A. Dictionaries and encyclopedias
   B. Handbooks and surveys
   C. Histories
   D. Theologies and harmonies
   E. Indexes and atlases

III. Language Aids
   A. Concordances
   B. Lexicons
   C. Word studies

The intended audience for this study guide is the average Christian lay-person in the church. Theologians, pastors, and professional Christian workers will presumably have passed far beyond the helps suggested in this chapter; but many Christians who sense their need of greater understanding of the Scriptures will welcome a brief mention of study aids that are readily available and do not require advanced training, a thorough knowledge of the Biblical languages, or a seminary education.

I. Study Bibles and Commentaries

A. Bibles. As indicated elsewhere, the Bible is its own best interpreter. Bible study begins with a good Bible. That is, a volume that is manufactured for hard use. Obtain a Bible with clear, large type and with wide margins. You will want to make many notes in the margins of the Bible, so use one with the widest margins possible. Your study Bible should be in the translation which will be most useful to you, probably the King James Version or the New American Standard Bible. It would be good, too, to use an edition which has cross-references included, whether in a center column, in the margins, or as footnotes. The use of those references will probably be explained in the introduction of your Bible. The Scofield Bible, for example, lists the next occurrence of a given referenced subject, and the first and last appearances of that subject. A great deal can be learned by the proper use of a cross-reference Bible without any other aids.

As your basic study Bible or as a companion work, you may want to consider one of the popular editions replete with references, footnotes, indexes, book introductions, glossaries, and so forth. In using such a work, however, you must keep in mind that the notes are always the work of an editor or an editorial committee whose theological bias will be reflected in the study aids. For example, the popular Scofield Bible has a strong dispensational approach to interpretation. If that's acceptable to you, you'll find it very helpful. If you have a differing interpretive view, you must keep that in mind as you use the helps. The Scofield Bible uses the King James Version, but the new edition corrects and updates the archaic words and expressions found in the older King James Version.

Other familiar study Bibles include the Pilgrim Bible, the Dickson Bible, the Thompson Bible, and, most recently, the Ryrie Study Bible. Charles Ryrie is a professor at Dallas Theological Seminary, and his work is conservative in interpretation, as one might expect. J. Vernon McGee of the "Through the Bible" radio broadcast is making a Bible available with his study notes included. Others are doing the same. So, there is no lack for helpful aids within the covers of a Bible itself to be used for study.

Along with a good work Bible, you will want to have various translations nearby, too. As discussed in chapter 6, there are numerous modern speech translations which you will find helpful in arriving at acceptable and useful ways of expressing Biblical truth. The comparison of several reliable translations will broaden your concept of various obscure or difficult passages.

B. Commentaries. For centuries, students of the Scriptures have been commenting on their understanding of God's revelation. Multitudes of commentaries are available, and you may profit by consulting them. However, you can't read everything written on a subject or a verse, nor should you; but you will want to discover a few that are particularly meaningful to you and are trustworthy. Commentaries come in multi-volumed sets on both Old and New Testaments, in single volumes on the whole Bible, or in sets or single books on various books or portions of the Bible. Before making a purchase of a large and expensive set, you would do well to give yourself a little time in looking around, consulting with your pastor or trusted students of the Word, using some in the church library, perhaps.

For a single volume on the entire Bible you might consider the Wycliffe Bible Commentary put out by Moody Press. Obviously, a single volume like this will not be able to comment on every verse or phrase of Scripture, so the particular item of your interest may not be included; but, generally, you'll find it helpful.

One caution needs to be raised in the use of commentaries. Our study of the Bible should begin and end with what the Bible says. It is its own best commentary. Avoid the temptation—especially when you need to prepare something on short notice—to consult the commentaries first and take their material before (or without) mastering the Biblical content.

A helpful guideline in determining which commentaries to consult is knowing something about the author and/or the publisher. The name of the publishing company may signal immediately that the volume is theologically biased—charismatic, covenant, ultra-dispensational, Roman Catholic, and so on. If you have found a particular author to be a blessing to you—G. Campbell Morgan, Griffith Thomas, or Harry Ironside, for example—you can consult his works with assurance of the kind of material and help you'll find in any of his volumes.

II. Reference Works

Just as the public or school library has a large section of reference works, so, thankfully, is there a large shelf of reference works available to the Bible student. This shelf will include Bible handbooks, Bible dictionaries, Bible histories, Bible introductions, surveys, indexes, theologies and books on doctrine, not to mention language aids which we'll discuss below.

A. Dictionaries and encyclopedias. A Bible dictionary is more than just a reference for correct spelling and definitions. It is more like an encyclopedia with explanations of the meanings of the terminology and vocabulary of Scripture. For example, a specific subject like "heaven" may be explained in several columns, including what the Old Testament teaches about heaven, what the New Testament teaches, what the history of the doctrine is, what the church has taught about it, what sources of information are available, and so forth. Customs and history, as well as doctrine, will be included in such references. *Unger's Bible Dictionary,* the *New Bible Dictionary,* the *Davis Bible Dictionary,* the *International Standard Bible Encyclopedia (ISBE)* are highly recommended volumes in this category.

Handbooks and surveys. A Bible handbook is a conglomeration of many facts and opinions which give helpful background to the Scriptures. Halley's and Unger's are two very popular volumes of this sort. In some respects, they are commentaries in miniature on the various books of the Bible with enlightening archeological and historical information included.

For a summary review of the various books of the Bible, surveys may be consulted. There are several good, concise surveys which present the basic theme of a book, a little of its background and author, perhaps, and comments on significant sections of the book, often providing an outline or analysis. Particularly helpful to this writer have been G. Campbell Morgan, *The Analyzed Bible;* Eric Hayden, *Preaching Through the Bible;* Henrietta Mears, *What the Bible Is All About;* and G. Coleman Luck, *The Bible Book by Book.*

C. Histories. To understand the customs and cultures of Biblical settings, one should read books on introduction to the Old or New Testaments, or Bible histories. Alfred Edersheim's two-volume sets are extremely important here: *Bible History—Old Testament* and *The Life and Times of Jesus the Messiah.* Sir William Ramsey's *St. Paul the Traveler and Roman Citizen* is unbeatable in its presentation of background material for the Book of Acts and the epistles of Paul.

D. Theologies and harmonies. More technical books on Bible interpretation (hermeneutics) and archeology would be of value to the serious student (also, books on doctrine and theology). One of the most helpful, but not new by any means, is William Evans, *The Great Doctrines of the Bible;* another is Lewis S. Chafer, *Major Bible Themes.*

The Gospels are unique in the Bible in that they cover the

same period of history and have the common purpose of presenting the life and ministry of Jesus, though from differing perspectives and to different audiences, to be sure. Since so much material is common to at least three, and sometimes all four of the Gospels, a useful volume for the student is A. T. Robertson's, *A Harmony of the Gospels.* In it are parallel columns enabling the reader to take one event and to see how it is described by each of the writers. At a glance, we can compare the use of words, details, reactions, and so on, and gain a composite picture of that event.

E. **Indexes and atlases.** Let's just make brief mention of various kinds of indexes which may be of value. *Nave's Topical Bible* lists the major references where particular subjects are discussed. Its use is obvious, as is the function of *The New Topical Text Book.* The *Treasury of Scripture Knowledge* contains 500,000 Scripture references and parallel passages arranged by chapter and verse. By using the cross-references, the patient student can bring all the weight of the Bible to bear upon a particular verse.

Finally, we must not overlook the value of good Bible maps. atlases, and charts. Many Bibles will have a section of maps at the back. This is probably the least-used portion of most peoples' Bible. Yet, they offer a lot of good help. In studying the wilderness wanderings of Israel or the missionary journeys of Paul, maps are indispensable. Relationships between Israel and contemporary nations can be better understood when their geographical proximity (or distance) is noted on a map. Maps of Palestine and Jerusalem in different historical periods are often included, and they enlighten the student as to the varying conditions under which the historical accounts occurred.

Study charts of the Bible are briefly discussed in another chapter, but the student may find the charts of Larkin and Humberd to be of great help in visualizing great doctrinal truths. Irving Jensen has published *Independent Bible Study* which teaches the use of charts in Bible study and teaching.

Visual aids of this sort, of course, are very profitable for analysis and comparison.

III. Language Aids

Since the setting of the Bible is not in western culture, we need the customs and culture studies as indicated above. Furthermore, the Scriptures were not written in English, but in languages foreign to us. Consequently, we need help in understanding the significance of the word choice, word order, and so forth, that is not always clearly reflected in the standard translations. Lest you be discouraged because you are not a Hebrew and Greek scholar, let me assure you that there are some excellent aids for the non-linguist. If used diligently, they can open up some of the hidden treasures of the Scriptures that are salted away in the ore of the original languages.

Hebrew has proved to be a difficult language for some students to master, while Greek is often more easily acquired with a little effort—at least a rudimentary knowledge of Biblical Greek. To accomplish this, of course, one would need some basic grammar books. Better yet, enroll in a Greek (or Hebrew) course at a nearby Bible institute, Bible college, or Christian liberal arts college.

A. Concordances. Without that knowledge of Greek and Hebrew, you can profitably study the Scriptures (though we certainly don't want to demean the value of knowing the original languages; in chapter 6 we quoted Robert Mounce, "Christian theology must never rest on the shaky foundation of being one language removed from the original. For maximum accuracy, revealed truth must be studied in the original languages"). To study the Bible without a knowledge of the original languages, you will need a few tools. You can begin with an English concordance to the Bible. A concordance is a listing of the words in the Bible with the references—book, chapter, and verse—where they occur. Many Bibles include small concordances at the back. They are incomplete, of course, but they do direct the seeker to some major texts on the most sought-after subjects. When you can't remember where a verse is in the Bible, you can locate it through a concordance if you can remember some key word. If you can remember only a common word, you may have to wade through long lists of references before you find the one you want.

The most helpful concordance to the serious student will be one that not only lists all the English words with all their occurrences—and, by the way, there are nearly 6,000 different words in the English Bible—but that indicates the different Greek or Hebrew words which the English term translates. It is not enough to know, for instance, that the word "love" appears in John 21 in three apparently identical questions of Jesus (verses 15, 16, 17). It is most significant that this one English word translates two different words in Greek. Not only that, but Peter's response to the Lord's first two questions, though translated "love" in English, are actually different words from that used by Jesus. Without that knowledge, the narrative appears to be almost useless repetition: "Do you love me?" "Yes, I love you." "Do you love me?" "Yes, I love you." "Do you love me?" "Yes, I love you."

Our point in this illustration is not to show what the significance of "love" is in John 21, but to show how important the proper concordance is for aid in Bible study. Two popular and monumental concordances which would show these distinctions in word origin are those commonly known as *Strong's* and *Young's*. Both are excellent, but each uses a different method of displaying its lists. Young's gives the English word in its heading and then divides the list into groups, indicating the various Hebrew or Greek word which is translated into that English term, pointing out also the significant differences in meanings. Then, all the references in that particular category are listed in order.

Strong's, on the other hand, uses a system of numbers with each reference which are listed at the back of the volume along with an explanation of what the original term was.

Either volume is helpful. It seems that one of them certainly must be in any student's library as an indispensable tool. By the way, these two concordances are for the King James Version of the Bible. As more and more versions are being used, it becomes more and more difficult to search out word references. Some publishers, however, are producing concordances to be used in connection with their own translations. And, there are some expanded concordances being produced which attempt to list the references in which related words appear from various translations. That's a difficult task, and the genius which produced electronic brains and computers will likely have to develop a programmed computer to bring order out of the potential chaos brought about by multitudes of translations.

B. Lexicons. For the student who knows at least a little Greek or Hebrew, a lexicon is an invaluable tool. A lexicon is simply a Greek or Hebrew dictionary which includes definitions, references to Scripture use, and extra-Biblical literary use. For Greek, *Thayer's Greek Lexicon* and the work of Arndt and Gingrich are, perhaps, the two most used by New Testament students in evangelical circles today.

C. Word studies. More helpful than lexicons to the non-linguistic student, however, are various word study books. Vincent, Robertson, and Wuest—and many others—have written volumes of work that attempt to explain the significance of the Greek terms in the New Testament in simple, non-technical language. Thus, they give word pictures that are of great value in understanding the New Testament.

This writer has found W. E. Vine's *Expository Dictionary of the New Testament* to be the single most valuable language tool in his library. This volume lists the major words of the New Testament—it is not exhaustive, by the way—and groups them according to the Greek word of which they are a translation. To refer to the illustration above, you would find in Vine's under the heading "Love": *agapao*—with appropriate comments as to its significance and explanations of various uses of it; *phileo*—with comments and explanations regarding its shades of difference and similarity. These happen to be verb forms, but you will find the related nouns in following paragraphs.

So, without a scholar's mastery of doctrine, linguistics, history, and so forth, the sincere believer who wants to know God's Word can discover something of the depths of divine revelation by careful study. Recognizing his dependence upon the Holy Spirit, using the Bible as his primary source, following acknowledged rules of interpretation, and referring to the aids available, he will rejoice in the treasures which he can be led to discover.

Let's get to work! "Study to shew thyself approved unto God, a workman that needeth not to be ashamed, rightly dividing the word of truth" (II Tim. 2:15).

10

How To Teach the Bible

   I. Choosing a Subject
      A. Consider the audience
      B. Bible passages
      C. Suggested topics

  II. Choosing a Method
      A. Audiovisuals
      B. Principles
      C. Cautions

 III. A Suggested Method
      A. Suggested lists
      B. An outline to follow
      C. An example

It is probably presumptuous to attempt in a single chapter a subject as large as teaching the Bible. Entire books have been written on the subject. In fact, professors may spend several semesters teaching numerous courses on how to teach the Bible effectively. Presumptuous or not, however, there may be some helpful ideas we can share in these few pages; and the examples we hope to present can be used by many of our readers with profit.

I. Choosing a Subject

The textbook is the Bible, but that's a large book with almost limitless approaches to its study; so the teacher will have to choose his subject first. It may be that the teacher is responsible for a Sunday School class or a youth fellowship or some other organized group of students for which a curriculum is established. If that's the case, the subject matter is already determined and the teacher must master that—determining, then, the method to use in its presentation.

A. Consider the audience. But, if the teacher must select his subject, he must give thought to several questions about his study group. What is their background for Bible study? What do they already know? Are they fairly well grounded in Biblical truth or are they novices? Do they have certain preconditioning that must be kept in mind? Are they from a Roman Catholic background, for instance, or charismatic, or from the drug culture, or are they highly sophisticated?

Is the study group a formal class situation, an informal home study, a group meeting or lunch break in the shop, an after-school fellowship, or what? All of these factors—and more, no doubt—will contribute to the wise choice of subject matter (and method).

B. Bible passages. A pretty safe subject in almost any situation is a Bible passage—a verse, a paragraph, a chapter. If you follow consecutively through a book of the Bible, you can avoid criticism for picking special subjects "aimed" at certain people or problems that are present in your group. After all, you can't be blamed for consistently pursuing an orderly study when you arrive at a controversial or "close to home" topic.

C. Suggested topics. If you're free to choose your own subject and there isn't some compelling reason for a particular topic or portion of Scripture, you might consider preparing a study that answers some pertinent question of the day, or one that is particularly suited for your group. Here are some suggestions:

What Does the Bible Teach about Abortion?
How Can a Person Know for Sure He's Saved?
Guidelines for Financial Planning
Priorities in the Home
Establishing a Personal Ethical Standard for Living in the Twentieth Century
The Role of the Church in Modern Society
Missions and the Lay Person

The list is merely suggestive, of course. How about these for further Biblical study ideas:

Six "Precious" Things in Peter's Letters
Seven "Walks" in Ephesians
Five "Much Mores" in Romans 5
The Phrase "In Christ" (used by Paul 80 times)
"The Fear of the Lord" in Proverbs

Surely, the list of subjects for Bible study groups is endless.

III. Choosing a Method

Both the subject and the audience must be kept in mind when selecting the method(s) to be used in teaching. Also, you have to consider what method(s) are suited to the teacher and for which adequate equipment is available. It's useless to plan to use a filmstrip as a teaching method if there is neither filmstrip, projector, nor screen available (or if it's an outdoor camp with no available electricity)!

A. Audiovisuals. Contrary to popular thought, audiovisuals are not intended primarily for children. Adults learn from audiovisuals, too. In fact, any successful salesman can tell you that he is constantly subjected to sales meetings where the latest in AV devices are used to "sell" him on his product, his opportunity, and the methods he can use to sell. The salesman, in turn, very likely will carry a catalog, or a loose-leaf binder with photos, or samples, or some other kind of "visual" to sell his product to the prospective buyer. He isn't necessarily aiming at children, either!

B. Principles. The principle that ought to guide the teacher in this area is that he is not teaching a *subject* so much as he is teaching *people!* So, the determination of a method ought to begin with the consideration of the students. What will help them learn the most effectively? How can they develop learning skills in the class? The subject must be considered, too, of course. Not every subject lends itself to role playing or drama, for example. Not everything can be taught by simple rote memorization.

Most of our adult Sunday School classes are probably taught by the lecture method. After all, that's what people have grown accustomed to over the years, and they do resist change. Not only that, but most teachers thrive in the position of authority; they delight in being the teacher while the rest of the group are learners. The teacher does his learning *before* class; the students are to learn *during* class. The reader can consult many fine teachers' manuals available today which will suggest a multitude of methods to involve the class in the learning process, so they learn more, and more effectively.

It would seem that in most every more or less formal class situation in our day, the teacher should have at his disposal certain basic teaching aids: an overhead projector, a black-board or drawing easel, slide and filmstrip projectors with adequate screens, and the like. These things, however, should never become the focus of attention. It isn't the clever audio-visual presentation that's your goal, it's learning—use whatever enhances learning!

C. Cautions. A caution or two might be in order. No one knows everything. No one can be expert in every field. Don't hesitate to call on others to assist you in your teaching task or even to substitute for you when you're dealing with a matter in which someone else is more knowledgeable or proficient. Team teach, in other words, where and when you can.

Also, beware of discussion just for the sake of discussion. It can degenerate into a "pooling of ignorance." After all, you're studying the Bible, and the Bible is authoritative. It doesn't rely upon the opinions of people. So, when you have discussion on the Bible, limit it to those who have studied the material or the passage, so they're not just speaking "off the top of their heads" (which may or may not be Spirit-controlled). Keep discussion on the point; don't embarrass anyone who tries to stray from the point, but keep to the issue at hand. If other interesting and worthwhile subjects come up, decide whether they are more important than what you're presently studying, or if they can be postponed for further study later.

For a very helpful method of personal study which can be used also in your own teaching, see Irving L. Jensen's two volumes: *Independent Bible Study* and *Enjoy Your Bible*. Mr. Jensen demonstrates how to create charts in Bible study which give permanent visual impact to a study of the Scriptures. You may enjoy this method of study and teaching.

III. A Suggested Method

We have certainly not touched all the methods of teaching the Bible; we've barely scratched the surface, to be sure. However, the writer wants now to demonstrate a method of Bible study and teaching which he has found to be helpful personally and well received in Bible studies he has conducted. This method was first suggested to him in a Bill Gothard seminar. It can be used without a deep background in Bible knowledge or training; it demands few tools but a little persistent study. It's also a fruitful method because there are so many subjects that lend themselves to it; furthermore, it takes one right into the Word itself to find the answers and the material.

There is no fancy name for it; it can be referred to simply as "studying lists in the Bible." The Bible is verbally inspired; that means that the very words of Scripture are significant. Why does a particular word occur where it does? Why that word instead of a synonym? The answer to both questions is that God saw to the choosing of the words He wanted in order to convey the specific ideas He wanted.

A. Suggested lists. The Bible is full of lists. Whenever you are reading and come across a list of any kind, pause to consider the context and then begin to study the list, word by word. What does each word mean? Is the order of the words significant? Do the terms build from lesser to greater? Or descend from higher to lower? Are they representative of steps of progress? Are they cumulative?

Here are some lists that you will find profitable to study— and to share in a teaching situation:

1. Exodus 20:3-17—The Ten Commandments, or God's Perfect Standard
2. Psalm 19:7-10—The Qualities and Benefits of God's Word
3. Proverbs 6:16-19—Seven Things God Hates
4. Matthew 5:3-12—The Beatitudes, or The Portrait of a Christian
5. Acts 2:42—The Program for the Church
6. Galatians 5:19-21—The Deeds of the Flesh
7. Galatians 5:22-23—The Fruit of the Spirit
8. II Timothy 3:16—What the Bible Is Good For
9. James 4:7-10—Steps In Overcoming Sin
10. II Peter 1:5-7—What Should Be Added to Faith

Well, there are many more, of course, but what is listed here is enough for many months of careful study.

B. An outline to follow. Although each study will take a little different direction because of the particular subject matter involved, there is a pretty consistent approach that you can take in your study.

1. First, list the words or terms as you find them in your English Bible.

2. Define the terms. A good dictionary or Bible word study book will be invaluable in this step.

3. Amplify the meaning by consulting related passages, other uses of the same word in the Bible, and so on. Here a good concordance is essential, especially one that shows the particular word being translated into the English. Consult other reliable translations so you get a good feeling of the key word. A volume like *Vine's Expository Dictionary of the New Testament* will be most helpful. Commentaries may be of help, too.

4. Find Biblical illustrations (especially biographical) that relate to the characteristic, event, or quality you're studying.

5. Determine whether the sequence of the terms is significant. What are the steps being illustrated? Do they build upon one another or amplify each other?

6. If necessary, rearrange the material you've compiled into a fashion more suitable for presentation to your particular study group.

Look back at No. 2 of the suggested lists above. Here's the way you might approach those verses in Psalm 19. In column one, list the six titles given to the Word of God (see below). In column two, list the qualities associated with those terms. In the third column, list the benefits promised. You'll have something like this (forget the terms in parentheses for the moment):

Names	Qualities	Benefits
1. Law of the Lord, v. 7 (principles) (instruction)	perfect (complete) (blameless)	converts the soul (changes the mind)
2. Testimony of the Lord, v. 7 (divine witness)	sure (firm) (reliable)	making wise the simple (guidance)
3. Statutes of the Lord, v. 8 (directions)	right (just) (fair)	rejoicing the heart (shine)

Names	Qualities	Benefits
4. Commandment of the Lord, v. 8 (decree)	pure (clear)	enlightening the eyes
5. Fear of the Lord, v. 9 (awareness)	clean (moral purity)	enduring forever (eternal)
6. Judgments of the Lord, v. 9 (decisions)	true (righteous) (trustworthy)	to be desired (v. 10)

Now you go back and fill in your amplifications of the terms, indicating what is the significant, the applicable, and so forth—striving for clarification. (We've put this step in parentheses in this chart.)

In suggestion No. 10 on page 116, it has been pointed out (probably by Gothard as well as others) that the list of virtues to be added to the believer's life begins with the root of faith and culminates with the fruit of the Spirit. One need add nothing to faith to be saved, for we are saved by faith alone; but once one has been saved, he is to grow in grace and knowledge, ultimately to be conformed to the image of Christ. The Peter passage shows the progress of that growth, listing the various "leaves" of the plant until the fruit is evidenced in its entirety in Christlikeness (such as described in another list in Galatians 5:22-23).

C. An example. Allow me to present in some detail a final "list study." This is an expanded study which includes, generally, the steps mentioned above but also adds some other features, notably a column of examples. In many studies it would be profitable to find examples solely from the life of Christ (consider that when studying the list of the fruit of the Spirit, for example).

THE PORTRAIT OF A CHRISTIAN (*The Beatitudes*) Matthew 5:3-12

Beatitude	Meaning and Amplification	Major Feature	Nature	Commitment to a God of —	Result	Examples
POOR IN SPIRIT v. 3	Spiritually destitute; Contrast: pride	Need	Emptiness for God	Domination	Receive the Kingdom of Heaven	Isaiah 6
THEY THAT MOURN v. 4	Lament, grieving, anguish over sin Contrast: "laugh now," Luke 6:25	Sorrow	Brokenness for God	Consolation	Comforted	Daniel Ezra
MEEK v. 5	Gentle, mild Contrast: self-interest	Selflessness	Selflessness for God	Vindication	Inherit the earth	Abraham, Gen. 13 Moses, Num. 12:3 with Ex. 32:32
HUNGER AND THIRST AFTER RIGHTEOUSNESS v. 6	Evidence of appetite Recognition of need for God's righteousness; righteousness = quality of being right or just	Spiritual appetite	Openness for God	Satisfaction	Filled = satisfied: contentment in God's will	Christ's desire to spend time alone with the Father Isa. 55:1-2 John 4:32
MERCIFUL v. 7	To feel sympathy, pity Tenderness demonstrated in action	Kindness	Tenderness for God	Benediction	Obtain mercy	Good Samaritan John 3:16 Romans 5:8
PURE IN HEART v. 8	Without blemish; no mixture Sincere Loyal	Cleanness	Holiness for God	Revelation	See God	Joseph could not be seduced Daniel would not be defiled Galatians 4:4
PEACEMAKERS v. 9	Not merely cessation of hostilities but harmonious relationships Rest, contentment	Harmony	Activeness for God	Approbation	Called sons of God	Paul to two women in Philippi Christ made peace with God possible
PERSECUTED	Suffering for righteousness'	Loyalty	Fearlessness	Compensa-	Rejoicing and	Paul

Well, there you have it. Ready to go teach a class now? Using the "list" method, as you can see, is a good way for private, personal study. It can also be done with someone else or in a class situation. Ask the class for suggestions of examples, for instance, or related Bible passages which come to their minds from their own study.

Need we say it in closing? The "Teacher" of any individual or group of believers must really be the Holy Spirit. He can, and does, use human instruments; but let's remind ourselves that that's all we are—instruments in His hands to be used to minister His Word to others. It's a grave responsibility, but a glorious privilege!

11

An Overview of the Bible – The Old Testament

I. Purpose for the Old Testament
   A. It is profitable
   B. It is preparatory

II. Order in the Old Testament
   A. Order changed
   B. Chronology

III. Survey of Old Testament Books
   A. The books of law
   B. The books of history
   C. The books of poetry
   D. The books of prophecy

The Old Testament is recognized by Christians as inspired by God and an integral part of His revelation. Yet, the New Testament gets the greater attention. Unfortunately, some parts of the Old Testament would probably not even be recognized by many when read to an audience of average churchgoers today. There is an appalling ignorance of Old Testament truth and its value. This can be overcome only by diligent study.

I. Purpose of the Old Testament

A. It is profitable. In writing to Timothy, Paul reminded him that the holy Scriptures which he had learned from childhood (and those would be the Old Testament books) were able to make him "wise unto salvation" (II Tim. 3:15). He goes on to say, then, that all Scripture came from God and is profitable (v. 16); his special application was, of course, to the Old Testament. So, we ought not to think that it is deficient in any way, nor that it is not applicable to us today. It most certainly is; and, when studied with and in light of the New Testament, it will yield God's full counsel. Do not neglect the Old Testament in your reading and study!

B. It is preparatory. Before we examine the grouping of the Old Testament books and the importance of their order, let's briefly consider why God gave us what we find in the Old Testament. In an earlier chapter, we noted that "The New Testament is in the Old Testament concealed, and the Old Testament is in the New Testament revealed." If the central theme of the Bible is Christ and His redemptive work, then the Old Testament can be regarded as the preparation for Him and His ministry. Its history brings events—religious, social, political, and so on—to the time of the coming of Christ. Its prophecy predicts His appearance and accomplishments. Its ceremonies point toward the meaning of His life, death, and achievement.

Speaking in a very practical manner, the New Testament also teaches us that the experiences of the Old Testament were not isolated events to be read and appreciated merely as historical occurrences. Rather, "all these things happened unto them *for ensamples:* and they are written for *our* admonition...." (I Cor. 10:11).

Much of the Old Testament law and ceremony has been superseded by Christ who came to fulfill it. No longer is it necessary to bring sacrifices of bulls and goats; no longer do we annually present a Passover lamb; the ceremonies and restrictions are not needed now. Does that mean they are of no value? Not at all; the study of those matters will reveal marvelous truths about God's dealings with men and, particularly, about the sufficient ministry of Christ on behalf of the believer. An Old Testament passage, as Dr. Jensen points out, may illustrate an aspect of salvation (as in the deliverance of the Exodus), or prophecy of it (as in Isaiah 53), or even state it explicitly (as in Genesis 16:6).

II. Order in the Old Testament

A. Order changed. The order in which we find the Old Testament books in our Bibles today is not exactly as it has always been. The Hebrew Bible placed some differently and in different order, often combining certain books, but the *content is the same,* and that's the important issue.

B. Chronology. One other comment must be made about the chronology of the Old Testament books. You will be completely befuddled and lose all sense of time, if you do not realize that the prophetic books have their setting within the context of the historical books. When you read the prophets— whether major or minor—you must realize that they lived, preached, and wrote during a particular historical era, and they had a particular audience in mind. For the sake of clarity, you should consult and use for constant reference a time chart such as John C. Whitcomb's "Chart of Old Testament Kings and Prophets." The introduction to the various prophetic books in a Bible like the Scofield Bible will suggest the audience and time period, too.

Israel's history in the Old Testament concludes with her scattered and separated. She had been taken into captivity many centuries earlier. Certain of the prophets wrote before her captivity, some during the period, and others after her return to the land. The following listing may help you keep a chronological bearing as you read the prophets:

Pre-exilic prophets: Jonah, Amos, Hosea, Obadiah, Joel, Isaiah, Micah, Jeremiah, Nahum, Zephaniah, Habakkuk

Exilic prophets: Ezekiel, Daniel

Post-exilic prophets: Haggai, Zechariah, Malachi

III. Survey of Old Testament Books

Space will not permit a detailed survey of each book, of course. In the previous chapter, several survey books were recommended which you will find helpful in getting an overview of the Old Testament, if you care to do so. Here we'll do scarcely more than give a sentence summary of the books.

A. The books of law. The historical books begin with the five books of the Law. They are referred to as the Pentateuch, which merely indicates that there are five such books in this section. Moses is the major author of all five. When seeing the books as a part of a group, we must not overlook the fact that each has a distinctive message. Redemption may be considered the general theme of this group, telling the story of Israel's redemption out of bondage into the Promised Land, but each of the books has a distinctive theme.

Genesis is the book of beginnings and explains the origin of the universe, the beginning of the human race, and the beginning of Israel. It introduces the patriarchs, and its history concludes in Egypt.

Exodus tells the story of the deliverance of Israel from Egypt. Moses is the human deliverer; to him God reveals His Law on Mt. Sinai. The 10 commandments and instruction regarding the building of the tabernacle are major features of the book.

Leviticus is a manual of worship, presenting the laws governing Israel. It reveals how a sinful people can approach a holy God, pointing to the coming of Jesus Christ, the "Lamb of God."

Numbers records Israel's 40 years of wilderness wanderings, the result of the nation's disobedience to God.

Deuteronomy means "second law" and includes the repetition of much of the law given in Exodus. The book warns and instructs the people in view of their approaching entrance into the Promised Land.

B. The books of history.

Joshua relates the conquest and division of Canaan, written by Joshua himself, the successor to Moses and a picture of Jesus (the Hebrew name "Joshua" being equivalent to the Greek name "Jesus").

Judges tells the awful story of Israel's sin, God's chastisement by means of oppressing nations, her repentance, and God's deliverance. This cycle is repeated seven times. The commentary on the people is repeated twice in the book, probably written by Samuel, "In those days there was no king in Israel, but every man did that which was right in his own eyes" (17:6, 21:25). God raised up judges who ruled the people and brought deliverance.

Ruth is the story of an ancestress of Christ who lived during the period of the judges. She was from Moab, but married an Israelite and chose to serve Israel's God. The book is a beautiful illustration of the Biblical concept of the "Kinsman-Redeemer" (for which see the appropriate note on p. 763 of the New Scofield Bible).

I, II Samuel tell the story of the beginnings of the monarchy of Israel. Samuel, prophet and judge, is the writer. The first book relates the reign of Saul, first king of Israel, and the succession of David to the throne. The second book spans the 40-year reign of David.

I, II Kings continue the history of the nation, carrying it beyond the pinnacle of fame and fortune under Solomon to the dividing of the nation into the northern kingdom (Israel) and the southern (Judah). The second book is important because of the historical setting it gives for the prophetical books later.

I, II Chronicles repeat the time span of the preceding three books, adding some details and repeating others. The reign of David and the preparations for building the temple are in I Chronicles, while the second book continues the narrative through Solomon's reign and then focuses on the southern kingdom. Its emphasis is on the religious, rather than the political, aspect of the history.

Ezra relates the return of the Jews from Babylonian captivity to rebuilding the temple in Jerusalem.

Nehemiah is a sort of sequel to Ezra; it reports on a second return to Jerusalem with a rebuilding of the city's walls. Jewish ordinances are reestablished in the land.

Esther narrates the exciting story of the deliverance of the Jews through the providential care of God (who is not mentioned in the book, by the way).

C. The books of poetry.

A few things should be noted about Hebrew poetry before a survey of the poetic books continues. There are at least four kinds of poetry in the Old Testament: *lyric*—the poetry of feeling (the song of Moses, Exodus 15, the Book of Lamentations, for examples); *didactic*—the poetry of instruction (like Proverbs, Ecclesiastes); *prophetic*—the poetry of prediction (the blessing of Jacob's sons, Genesis 49; the suffering servant, Isaiah 53); *dramatic*—the poetry of drama (Job, the Song of Solomon).

The reader may be disappointed in reading the Biblical poetic books, if he expects them to read like poetry in English. Before many of the proverbs and psalms can be fully appreciated, the student needs to understand something about *parallelism*. We are most familiar with parallelism in sound, that is, a rhyme of sounds: blue and true, green and keen, goat and boat, and so forth. But Hebrew poetry uses a rhyme of ideas. Although there are at least three kinds of parallelism in Hebrew poetry, you will not need a deep study to recognize and appreciate their appearance. One kind of parallelism (rhyme in idea) occurs when the second part of a sentence or clause agrees or develops the first. Example: Psalm 92:12—

"The righteous shall flourish like the palm tree:" (1)

"he shall grow like a cedar in Lebanon." (2)

These two ideas are parallel—not identical, but conveying the same idea. Another example is Psalm 140:1—

"Deliver me, O Lord, from the evil man;" (1)

"preserve me from the violent man;" (2)

A second kind of parallelism is when two parts are set in contrast, such as in Psalm 34:10—

"The young lions do lack, and suffer hunger:" (1)

"but they that seek the Lord shall not want any good thing." (2)

Or, Isaiah 65:13-14—

"Behold, my servants shall eat," (1)

"but ye shall be hungry:" (2)

"behold, my servants shall drink," (1)

"but ye shall be thirsty:" (2)

"behold, my servants shall rejoice," (1)

"but ye shall be ashamed:" (2)

"Behold, my servants shall sing for joy of heart," (1)

"but ye shall cry for sorrow of heart," (2)

Constructive parallelism is a third kind. Here, ideas are built upon successively until a united, complete idea is expressed. You can see this in Psalm 1:3—"And he shall be like a tree planted by the rivers of water,"

"that bringeth forth his fruit in his season" (1)

"his leaf also shall not wither:" (2)

"and whatsoever he doeth shall prosper." (3)

Here's another illustration: Proverbs 9:1-2—

"Wisdom hath builded her house," (1)

"she hath hewn out her seven pillars:" (2)

"She hath killed her beasts;" (3)

"she hath mingled her wine;" (4)

"she hath also furnished her table." (5)

There is one more type of Hebrew poetry that must be mentioned. It is not unique to Hebrew literature, however.

That is acrostic or alphabetic poetry—lines or verses beginning with separate letters of the alphabet in order. Of course, these will not be apparent in a translation. You can seldom translate from one language to another using words which begin with the same letters in the second language as they do in the first. Therefore, acrostic or alphabetic poems in the Hebrew Bible do not appear to be so in English. Notice, however, that the first 2 and last 2 chapters of Lamentations contain just 22 verses. There are 22 letters in the Hebrew alphabet, and the verses of these chapters begin with the various letters of the alphabet in order. The third chapter has 66 verses, and there are 3 verses for each letter! Try writing some poetry like that and see how well you do. It's a very helpful device for memorization, by the way, and that's probably the reason it is used so often in the Bible.

The prime example of the alphabetic poem is Psalm 119. In many versions of the English Bible this feature is conveyed by the division of the chapter into 22 sections of 8 verses each. All 8 verses in each section begin with the same letter of the Hebrew alphabet and each section appears in alphabetical order! Imagine writing a poem with 8 verses starting with "A," 8 more with "B," and right on through. Many Bibles, by the way, indicate before each section the particular Hebrew letter for each section, such as "Aleph, Beth, Gimel," and so on.

Now, study these books of poetry with a greater appreciation of their literary and spiritual content.

Job is the dramatic story of a believer, probably living in the time of Abraham, whose personal experience demonstrates how the righteous meet the problem of human affliction. After the advice and counsel of human wisdom, God reveals something of Himself and His sovereignty. The book deals with the question of why the righteous suffer.

Psalms is a collection of 150 devotional poems, prayers, and songs. At least half were written by David. Many reveal the believer's communion with God. Some are messianic;

that is, they have reference to Christ.

Proverbs is a collection of practical maxims for daily life originating in divine wisdom. Solomon wrote most of them. A practice of reading one chapter of Proverbs each day will provide a great deal of help for the believer in his daily experience, and it will be repeated each month.

Ecclesiastes clearly emphasizes the futility of life apart from God. The human viewpoint of things is shown to be shortsighted and vain. Solomon, who was the wisest of men, is the human author.

Song of Solomon is a romantic tale from the experience of Solomon, no doubt. It has been subjected to many interpretations from Bible students, including its representation of God's love for Israel and its foreview of Christ and the Church.

D. The books of prophecy. A few remarks about these books and about the ministry of prophets will aid the student in understanding this important section of the Old Testament. A prophet, strictly speaking, is one who speaks in the place of, or on behalf of, another. He may or may not predict future events, but he does always speak to men for God. In the Old Testament, prophets were men raised up by God in times of declension and apostasy in Israel—when both priest and king were no longer worthy channels for the expression of God. They were the evangelists of their day, the revivalists and patriots.

The prophets must be considered according to their relationship to the captivity of the nation of Israel. Those who wrote prior to the captivity are called pre-exilic prophets; that group included Obadiah, Joel, Jonah, Amos, Hosea, Isaiah, Micah, Nahum, Jeremiah, Zephaniah, and Habakkuk. The exilic prophets were Jeremiah, Daniel, and Ezekiel; while Haggai, Zechariah, and Malachi prophesied after the exile. The period of the prophets covered 500 years, from the ninth to the fourth centuries B.C. From that time on, they were silent until John the Baptist.

There were largely three elements in the message of the prophets: 1) they spoke to their own age, directly from God: repent! 2) they predicted future events: judgment, Messiah. 3) they preached living messages to our own age— eternal principles of right and wrong. The fulfillment of their predictive prophecies had a twofold character—that which was local and for the prophet's time, and that which was predictive of the future, particularly in relation to Christ and to the nation Israel. It is important to note that the Church is not in the prophets at all. This is the "mystery" that God kept until He wished it to be revealed (Eph. 3:3, 11, 12).

The "Major" Prophets are not more important than the "Minor"; they are usually just considerably longer. The first 5 are major; 12 are minor.

Isaiah writes to the southern kingdom and warns of coming judgment. The book is a miniature in some senses: chapters 1-39 emphasize the judgment of God; chapters 40-66, His comfort and mercy. The prophecy is replete with messianic references.

Jeremiah is sometimes called the "weeping prophet" because his colorful message is one of doom; his counsel was often unpopular; he decried the backsliding of the nation.

Lamentations, besides being acrostic, is Jeremiah's lament over Jerusalem's destruction by Babylon; it illustrates God's sorrow over His need to chastise His people.

Ezekiel is a highly prophetic book written in mystical metaphors; the prophet foretells Jerusalem's doom and, also, her future restoration.

Daniel contains a good deal of personal history during the captivity of God's people, beginning in Babylon. The prophecies are fundamental to an understanding of God's program in the future. Without its teaching, one would be lost in understanding Bible prophecy in general, and the Book of the Revelation in particular.

Hosea, writing during the same time as Isaiah, tells of

Israel's unfaithfulness, chastisement, and restoration. It apparently was the literal experience of Hosea to marry a woman who became unfaithful, went into prostitution, but was ultimately restored to him; throughout it all, he loved her. It is a powerful illustration of God's forgiving love for His people.

Joel calls for repentance in Judah in light of the coming "Day of the Lord," foreshadowed by a plague of locusts.

Amos, like the rest of the prophets, preaches messages that are suitable for preaching today. He proclaims God's inevitable judgment upon sin to a generation which was prosperous materially, but destitute morally.

Obadiah picks out a particular nation, other than Israel, and tells of God's forthcoming judgment upon Edom, who had descended from Esau and was no friend to the Jews.

Jonah is, no doubt, the most familiar and questioned prophecy of all, not because of the message, but because of the extraordinary experience of the prophet. Nonetheless, it's the true story of a reluctant missionary who finally sees the Assyrian capital of Nineveh repent and turn to God.

Micah is most noted for his prediction of the birthplace of Messiah 700 years in advance. He preaches strongly against Israel's sins.

Nahum followed Jonah by about 150 years. Whereas Ninevah was spared as the result of Jonah's preaching, Nahum foretells the coming destruction of the city.

Habakkuk introduces a statement that will be repeated three times in the New Testament: "the just shall live by his faith" (2:4; cf. Rom. 1:17; Gal. 3:11; Heb. 10:38). It is made even more emphatic by the teaching of this prophet which shows God's plan to punish a sinful nation by an even more sinful one.

Zephaniah accents the same theme as Joel when he relates the judgment of Judah to the future "Day of the Lord."

Haggai prophesied in the days of Ezra and the rebuilding

of the temple after the exile. He pleads for the taking up of the work of rebuilding.

Zechariah is parallel to Haggai in that he, too, urges that the temple be rebuilt; but his prophecy is most noted for his visions of the ultimate triumph of God's kingdom. He foretells both Messiah's first and second comings.

Malachi concludes the prophecies of the Old Testament and looks forward to John the Baptist and Christ, who were not to come until after 400 years of silence from God. He pleads for reform before Messiah comes.

12

An Overview of the Bible – The New Testament

    I. Purpose for the New Testament
       A. Relationship to the Old Testament
       B. Applying New Testament principles

   II. Order in the New Testament
       A. Groupings
       B. Analysis

  III. Survey of New Testament Books
       A. The Gospels and Acts
       B. The Epistles
       C. The Revelation

The Old Testament lays the foundation for the New—historically, politically, socially, culturally, and religiously. The Old Testament books are picture books, filled with symbols, types, and narratives which illustrate the great theological truths enacted and expounded in the New Testament.

Some teachers have found interesting parallels between the Testaments. Robert Campbell, for example, shows a correspondence between the five books of the law and the groupings of the New Testament books:

The Gospels correspond to Genesis—the beginning of things

Acts corresponds to Exodus—God leading His people from the bondage of the law to the freedom of grace

The Pauline epistles correspond to Leviticus—teaching service, worship, and the position of saints

The general epistles correspond to Numbers—revealing the trials and sufferings of the pilgrimers

The Revelation corresponds to Deuteronomy—giving God's prophetic Word in regard to Jews, Gentiles, and God's people.

J. R. W. Stott puts it well in summarizing the New Testament: "It is a fascinating tale of the words and deeds of Jesus of Nazareth, first of what He 'began to do and teach' during His life on earth and then of what He continued to do and teach through His chosen apostles after the Lord returned to His Father and constituted His church." (*Understanding the Bible*, p. 114)

I. Purpose for the New Testament

The Stott quotation pretty well sums up the content of the New Testament. Unger shows how the central theme of Christ is demonstrated in its content:

In the Gospels Christ is *manifested* to the world and His gospel *provided* in the death, resurrection, and ascension of the Redeemer. In the Acts Christ is *proclaimed* and His gospel is *propagated* in the world. In the epistles His gospel is *expounded* in its doctrinal and practical meaning. In the Apocalypse all the redemptive purposes of God in and through the Redeemer are *consummated* for time and eternity. (*Unger's Bible Handbook*, p. 463)

A. Relationship to the Old Testament. Griffith Thomas described the Old Testament as "a book of unfulfilled prophecies, unexplained ceremonies, unsatisfied longings. The Christ of the New Testament fulfills the prophecies, explains the ceremonies, satisfies the longings." He shows the relationship, also, with a simple chart:

Old Testament	*New Testament*
Foundation	Superstructure
Foreshadow	Fulfillment
Promise	Performance
Commencement	Consummation

B. Applying New Testament principles. Since we are living in the same age (the age of Grace or the Church), it may be somewhat easier for us to apply the New Testament to our lives than the Old. There are certain kinds of writing included, and here are some suggestions for applying them:

1. Teachings and commandments—usually the applications are clear and direct. For example, "Let us love one another" (I John 4:7). The epistles present a great deal of this kind of material.

2. History—avoid the sins related in the narratives, and follow the examples given. There are many such portions in the Gospels and Acts.

3. Testimony, found especially in the epistles—brings encouragement to the believer whose response will be to join in agreement.

4. Prophecy occurs throughout the New Testament but especially in the Revelation. Not only do we learn what God's plan is for His people in particular and the world in general, but the study of prophecy provides an incentive to righteous living. "Seeing then that all these things shall be dissolved, what manner of persons ought ye to be in all holy conversation and godliness, looking for and hasting unto the

coming of the day of God . . .?" (II Peter 3:11-12). (Based on Irving L. Jensen: *Enjoy Your Bible*, pp. 124-125)

II. Order in the New Testament

There is order and arrangement in the New Testament, of course, as there was in the Old. To some degree, the books are chronological. The events of Acts do follow the events of the Gospels. The Revelation does reveal the end times, and the epistles are interwoven in the time span of the Acts and following.

A. Groupings. Here are two groupings of the New Testament books which will enable you to get an overview of their content at a glance:

1. Historical—

5 books
  4 Gospels and Acts

2. Biographical—

4 books
  4 Gospels

Historical—
1 book
  Acts

Doctrinal and practical—
21 books
  Pauline and general epistles

Pedagogical—
21 books
  Epistles

Prophetical—
1 book
  Revelation

Prophetic—
1 book
  Revelation

B. Analysis. Another chart may prove to be helpful. This one, suggested by Robert Campbell, pulls together a number of analyses of the New Testament and tells a lot about the content of the various sections:

	1.	2.	3.	4.	5.	6.
GOSPELS	Historical	Past	Christ	Christ as Prophet	Israel	John 14:26
ACTS			Church	Christ as Priest	Church	John 16:13a
EPISTLES	Doctrinal	Present				
REVELATION	Prophetical	Future	Consummation	Christ as King	World	John 16:13b

Explanation:

1. The four major groupings of the New Testament books are listed according to the character of their content. Note that both the Gospels and Acts are largely historical.

2. Here the groups are divided according to the time of their application. While some of the content of each group may include time references outside what is indicated in the chart, this is their major reference. The events recorded in the Gospels and Acts are past history. While the events of the epistles are also past, their doctrinal teaching and practical application continue throughout this present age. The early chapters of Revelation occurred in the past, but the major thrust of the book is prophetical—regarding events yet future in fulfillment.

3. Column three indicates the major subject material of the groupings. Here, Acts is included with the epistles, for all those books deal largely with the church; while the Gospels related the experiences of Christ, and the Revelation points to the consummation of all things.

4. Since Christ is to be seen in all the Scriptures, if we divide the New Testament books into the groupings indicating the particular aspect of Christ that they emphasize, you have the viewpoints listed in column four.

5. Considering the three segments of people in the world, these groupings indicate the particular segment to which the content may be applied. In the Gospels there is considerable material dealing with the nation of Israel; the prophecies of the latter chapters of Matthew, for example, tell about Israel's future in the end times. Furthermore, Jesus came to present Himself to Israel as their Messiah, and the Gospels make that presentation (and their rejection) as a major theme. The Acts and epistles, again, deal with the church; while the Revelation includes both Israel and the church but, also reveals what is to transpire for the world as a whole including the unbelieving world outside the church and Israel.

6. The references in John's Gospel indicate the source of the revelation included in the various groupings and the role of the Holy Spirit in these groupings. The Gospels are recorded by the disciples who lived and ministered with Christ and to whom the Holy Spirit would "bring all things to your remembrance, whatsoever I have said unto you," (John 14: 26) enabling them to give an accurate account. The apostles gave us the epistles under the direction of the Holy Spirit who, Jesus said, "when he, the Spirit of truth, is come, he will guide you into all truth: for he shall not speak of himself; but whatsoever he shall hear, that shall he speak . . . ." (John 16:13). Regarding prophecy (such as the Revelation), Jesus promised "and he will shew you things to come" (John 16:13).

III. Survey of New Testament Books

A. The Gospels and Acts. The Gospels record the appearance in human history and within the Hebrew nation of the promised Messiah, Jesus Christ, and tell the wonderful story of His manifestation to Israel, His rejection by that people,

His crucifixion, resurrection, and ascension. As Unger says:

[They] are neither histories of the life of Christ nor biographies. They are rather portraits of the person and work of the long-promised Messiah, Israel's King and the world's Savior. As portraits they present four different poses of one unique personality. Matthew, by the Holy Spirit, presents Christ as King, Mark as Servant, Luke as Man, and John as God . . . . The gospels are designedly incomplete as a story, but marvelously complete and purposeful as a divine revelation of the Son of God our Savior! (*Unger's Bible Handbook,* pp. 465-66)

The same writer presents a useful chart indicating the various differences in emphasis and purpose among the gospel accounts (p. 467):

MATTHEW	MARK	LUKE	JOHN
The Prophesied King	The Obedient Servant	The Perfect Man	The Divine Son
Lionlike	Oxlike	Manlike	Eaglelike
Prophetic	Practical	Historical	Spiritual
To the Jew	To the Roman	To the Greek	To the Church
The Davidic King	The Servant of the Lord	The Son of Man	The Word of God
David's Righteous Branch Jer. 23:5-6	My Servant the Branch Zech. 3:8	The Man the Branch Zech. 6:12	The Branch of the Lord Isa. 4:2
Official			Personal
King	Servant	Son of Man	Son of God
Synoptic			Supplementary
Outward, public, Galilean, earthly			Inward, private, Judean, heavenly

Matthew was written to prove the messiahship of Jesus; it emphasizes Him as King, describing His arrival and His ultimate rejection. Quoting heavily from the Old Testament, it is directed especially to the Jews.

Mark is the most concise of the Gospels. It begins with Christ's ministry, not His birth; directed largely to the Romans, it emphasizes His supernatural powers.

Luke is the most historically detailed Gospel; it emphasizes Jesus' compassion for poor, sinful humanity. He is the perfect man, the Saviour for imperfect men.

John is distinct from the other three Gospels, though it harmonizes with them. John's emphasis is upon the deeper spiritual meaning of Christ's teaching and ministry. He is presented, not only as man, but as the Son of God.

Acts stands with the Gospels as a book of history, but separated from them because it does not include the life and ministry of Christ—except in His brief post-resurrection appearances prior to the ascension.

Acts records the descent of the Holy Spirit, and the beginning of a new thing in human history, the church. The division of the race now becomes threefold—Jew, Gentile, and the church of God. Just as Israel is in the foreground from the call of Abram to the resurrection of Christ, so now the church fills the scene from the second chapter of Acts to the fourth chapter of the Revelation.

("History, Facts, and Worth of the Bible," New York Bible Society)

As indicated in an earlier statement, the Gospels record what Christ began to do and teach; Acts continues His ministry through His apostles, empowered by the Holy Spirit.

B. The Epistles. Epistles are letters. This is the form that much of the New Testament took. As the apostles wrote to the newly forming churches, giving counsel, resolving problems, admonishing godly living, the Holy Spirit directed their writing, revealing to them what should be included, and preserving these letters for the benefit of the church down through the centuries. The Apostle Paul is the author of at least 13 of them (from Romans through Philemon); these are addressed to actual churches or persons of the first century.

Many Bible scholars believe that Paul also wrote the Epistle to the Hebrews which is not addressed to a particular individual or church, and which is presented anonymously. Certainly, it is Pauline in much of its content and style.

The remaining seven epistles are called "general epistles" because they are not entitled with the name of a specific church or person to whom they are written. Rather, they all bear the name of their human author. At times, critics like to point out supposed contradictions between the writers of the various epistles. Like all such criticisms—whether of Old Testament books or New—careful study will usually resolve the apparent conflict. For example, if you keep in mind the purpose and emphasis of a writer, you may be able more easily to understand his teaching in relation to the teachings of other writers. Keep these facts in mind, for example:

Paul emphasized Christian doctrine, insisting on faith.

James emphasized Christian practice, insisting on works.

Peter emphasized Christian trials, insisting on hope.

John emphasized Christian experience, insisting on love.

Romans has been called "the first Christian theology"; it clearly reveals God's plan of salvation and its application to everyday life. It is foundational to the rest of Paul's epistles.

I Corinthians deals with problems in a local church: disunity, immorality, church disorder. Important instruction is given regarding spiritual gifts, resurrection, love, and church order.

II Corinthians vindicates the ministry of Paul and his apostleship and includes teaching on Christian stewardship.

Galatians is particularly directed to the problem of Judaizers, those who try to bring Jewish Christians back under the law. Justification by faith is a theme echoing Romans.

Ephesians presents the glory of the Church, pointing to its breaking down of human barriers (Jew vs. Gentile) and its illustration in marriage.

Philippians emphasizes joy in the Christian experience,

to be found in following the example of Christ and in putting full trust in the wisdom and provision of God.

Colossians is a marvelous treatise on Christ and His supremacy; it was written to combat the false teaching which denied Christ's deity. Paul shows Him to be Head of the church—and the whole universe.

I Thessalonians counsels a local church regarding Christian living. An interesting feature of the letter is that each of its five chapters concludes with some reference to the second coming of Christ.

II Thessalonians is a sequel to the first letter, giving further clarification about the second coming and warning against certain sinful practices.

I Timothy is the first of three letters referred to as the "pastoral epistles" because they include so much advice for young ministers of the Lord. The emphasis is on sound doctrine and good church government.

II Timothy warns about apostasy which had already begun, and emphasizes the place of the Word of God as authoritative in the church. This was the last letter written by Paul before his death.

Titus, the final of the pastorals, is addressed to a trusted pastor in Crete, again emphasizing sound doctrine and godly living.

Philemon is the most personal of Paul's letters. It is written to intercede on behalf of a runaway slave who had become converted. It aptly illustrates the doctrine of imputation in Paul's willingness to have the slave's debt "charged to my account."

Hebrews demands a knowledge of the Old Testament ceremonies and order for full understanding. The writer demonstrates the superiority of Jesus Christ to all the demands, ceremonies, and ordinances of the Old Testament. He is the Great High Priest to which the Old Testament ceremony pointed.

James, written by a brother of Jesus, emphasizes the

practical nature of Christian faith, demanding works as an evidence of genuine faith.

I Peter is a letter of encouragement to Christians scattered throughout Asia Minor because of persecution, warning against the enemy without.

II Peter warns against the enemy within the church—false teaching. Peter wrote the letter shortly before his death, and it is similar in content to Paul's last letter (II Timothy).

I John, like Colossians, is written to combat theological error regarding the deity of Christ. His message is to believers of varying stages of spiritual maturity, urging them to deeper spiritual knowledge and to the continual practice of brotherly love. He emphasizes the assurance of eternal life for true believers.

II, III John are brief letters of warning; the one against fellowship of any kind with false doctrine and its teachers, the other against refusing fellowship with those who are true believers. "Close the door" to false teachers, he says, but "open the door" to fellow Christians.

Jude, like II Peter, is a sharp warning against false teachers and apostasy.

C. The Revelation. Often this book of the Bible will be referred to by its Latin name, the Apocalypse. In either case, the name refers to the revealing or unwrapping of something that has been hidden—and this final book surely does that! It is certainly the "capstone of Biblical prophecy." The key to the book's content is to be found in verse 19 of chapter 1: "Write the things which thou hast seen" (chapter 1); "and the things which are" (chapters 2-3); "and the things which shall be hereafter" (chapters 4-22).

Amplifying the prophecy of Daniel and other Old Testament passages, Revelation presents the climactic events of world history in a series of prophetic visions leading to the final conflict between right and wrong and the ultimate triumph of God's will.

13

You and Your Bible

I. Your Knowledge of the Bible
  A. Testing your knowledge
  B. Using your knowledge

II. The Value of the Bible to You
  A. It works for you
  B. It aids you
  C. It's your manual

III. The Value of the Bible through You
  A. The best translation
  B. Adorning Scripture

If the Bible is what we say it is—the inspired revelation of Almighty God—and, if its purpose is to convert, transform, comfort, train, and equip the Christian, then the Bible-believer should be characterized by a thorough knowledge of the book and a life that reflects its teachings. Unfortunately, such is not always the case.

I. Your Knowledge of the Bible

A. Testing your knowledge. Try this test to check up on your own knowledge of the Bible. Don't look at the answers (which appear at the end of the chapter) until you've done your best to answer all the questions.

Fill in the blanks.

Bible People

1. _____ took Daniel to Babylon.
2. Jacob's first wife was _____ .
3. _____ was the first high priest of Israel.
4. The father of the Jews was _____ .
5. Who was given a coat of many colors? _____
6. _____ made an axe head float on water.
7. _____ lifted a brazen serpent on a pole in the camp of Israel.
8. Who defeated a whole army while leading only 300 men? _____
9. _____ delivered the message at Pentecost.
10. _____ and Paul sang at midnight while in prison.
11. David's second son by Bathsheba was named _____
12. _____ slew a thousand enemies with a jawbone.
13. Name the son of David's enemy-king who was his closest friend _____
14. Cupbearer of King Artaxerxes who helped rebuild the wall _____
15. _____ was a young boy, serving in the

temple, when God called him.

16. From the cross, Jesus entrusted his mother into _____'s care.
17. _____ , a deacon, was stoned to death in Saul's presence.
18. _____ led the children of Israel across the Jordan River.
19. Name the king who killed James, the brother of John _____
20. A herdsman who became an Old Testament prophet was _____ .

Bible Dates and Places

21. The home of Mary and Martha was at _____ .
22. Mount _____ was the setting for Elijah's "fire" sermon.
23. The place of Christ's first miracle was _____ .
24. On what mountain was the law given to Moses? _____ _____
25. _____ was the city where Achan stole the Babylonian garment.
26. Jesus was going through _____ when he met the woman at the well.
27. Philip explained the Gospel to an eunuch from _____ _____.
28. Joseph became a great man in _____ .
29. The battle between Christ and the armies of antichrist will be fought in the Valley of _____ .
30. John was on the Isle of _____ when he saw the vision of the Revelation.

Bible Objects

31. Paul escaped from Damascus by going over the wall in a _____ .
32. Aaron had a _____ that budded.
33. For a portion of _____ , Esau sold his birthright.

34. God sent a _____ to swallow one of His prophets.
35. God sent _____ daily to feed the Israelites in the wilderness.

Now those questions were not particularly doctrinal or relevant to godly living, so much as they comprised a simple checkup on Bible knowledge. To ascertain further your workable knowledge of the Word, consider these questions: where would you look in the Bible to find:

1. the 10 commandments?
2. the story of the prodigal son?
3. the key chapter on the subject of the resurrection?
4. the key chapter on the rapture of the church?
5. the parables of the kingdom of heaven?
6. the story of the fall of man—his first encounter with sin?
7. the feeding of the 5,000?
8. the Sermon on the Mount?
9. the prophecy concerning the suffering servant?
10. the prophecy of the 70 weeks?

B. Using your knowledge. To be more practical, perhaps, how would you go about helping a friend who needed counsel regarding:

1. the plan of salvation?
2. the problems of fear and anxiety?
3. marriage?
4. temptation?
5. God's will?
6. personality conflicts?
7. speaking in tongues?
8. baptism?

Now all of these questions have been offered merely to emphasize the importance of *knowing* the Word of God and causing the reader to evaluate his/her knowledge of what he/she claims to be so important to him/her. William Lyon Phelps once said, "I believe a knowledge of the Bible is more valuable than a college course without the Bible." He was depreciating higher education but expressing priorities; if you can't have both, take the Bible—it's essential.

II. The Value of the Bible to You

If you've come along with us this far through this study guide, perhaps what follows may not seem so important to you. Surely, you recognize the value of the Bible to you. Many have willingly chosen to give up their lives rather than give up the Bible, because they considered it invaluable to you.

A. It works for you. Perhaps it's too obvious and simple to point out that the Bible contains light to direct you, food to feed you, and comfort to cheer you. It's the traveler's map, the pilgrim's staff, the pilot's compass, the soldier's sword, the Christian's charter. It should fill your memory, rule your heart, and guide your feet. Whatever your experience or place in life, the Bible is appropriate and relevant. As Irving Jensen puts it:

> In its work of diagnosis the Word exposes the cancer of sin and brings conviction (Heb. 4:12-13). In its healing work it cleans and purifies (John 15:3; 17:17; Eph. 5:25-26). Its manna gives strength for living (Deut. 8:3), and its sword equips for battle (Eph. 6:17). As a manual it gives counsel for our walk (Ps. 119:24), and as waters flowing from the throne of God it brings forth fruit to the glory of God (Ps. 1:2-3). (Irving Jensen: *Enjoy Your Bible*, p. 117)

B. It aids you. Someone has compiled a list of circumstances of life and the passages which will prove to be helpful in those circumstances. Perhaps you can use these in your own life or in counseling someone else.

When in sorrow, read John 14.

When men fail you, read Psalm 27.

When you have sinned, read Psalm 51.

When you worry, read Matthew 6:19-34 and Philippians 4:4-7.

When you are in danger, read Psalm 91.

When you have the blues, read Psalm 34.

When God seems far away, read Psalm 139.

When you are discouraged, read Isaiah 40.

When doubts come upon you, try John 7:17.

When you are lonely or fearful, read Psalm 23.

When you forget your blessings, read Psalm 103.

When your faith needs stirring, read Hebrews 11.

When you feel down and out, read Romans 8:31-39.

When you need courage for your task, read Joshua 1.

When the world seems bigger than God, read Psalm 90.

When you want rest and peace, read Matthew 11:25-30.

When you want Christian assurance, read Romans 8:1-30.

When you grow bitter or critical, read I Corinthians 13.

When your prayers grow narrow or selfish, read Psalm 67.

If you want to be fruitful, read John 15.

Before church service, read Psalm 84.

To find the secret of happiness, read Colossians 3:12-17.

When you leave home for work or travel, read Psalm 121.

To learn how to get along with people, read Romans 12.

In considering investments and returns, read Mark 10:17-31.

To discover true worship, read Isaiah 58:1-12.

To see the prophets' idea of religion, read Isaiah 1:10-18; Micah 6:6-8.

One very important value of the Bible is its strength to help in times of temptation. Christ's encounter with Satan illustrates this strength of the Word. Cheever puts it this way:

It was by such use of God's Word that our Lord put Satan to flight, and not by any array of angels or any exercise of supernatural power, but by doing what He knew to be the will of God, as it was written . . . . He simply smote him with the sword of the Spirit, which is the Word of God, and that was enough. He used no other argument, no other compulsion than that of divine truth . . . . It was an example for us all, for the ministry, for the churches, in the conflict against sin and Satan. We must throw ourselves on God's Word, and use it, and apply it, not as the word of man, but as it is in truth, the very Word of God only. We are not to be afraid of it .... we are not to doubt it, we are not to withhold it, nor conceal it, we are neither to suffer its perversion, nor to thrust it as a sword into the scabbard, instead of into men's hearts and iniquities, but we are to draw it forth and smite with it on every side. Neither man's expediency nor permission is to be the rule, but only God's Word. (George B. Cheever, "God's Timepiece for Man's Eternity")

As you are reading or studying Scripture, there are three questions you should continually ask: 1) what does it say?—that's observation; 2) what does it mean?—that's interpretation; and 3) what does it mean to me?—that's application. The facts of Scripture are true, but of limited value unless they are applied personally.

C. It's your manual. The Bible, after all, is man's living manual. When you buy an automobile or a washing machine, you receive a manual of operation for the machinery. It tells you how to operate it, how to service it, how to make necessary adjustments, what to look for if trouble develops, and so forth. The Bible is like that. Remember that the same breath of God that brought man into being (Gen. 2:7) brought the Word into being (II Tim. 3:16). To ignore the operator's manual is to court trouble with the new car you've bought; to ignore the Word of God is to face certain disaster with the life that's been entrusted to you—yours! God is the Master Mechanic; He made us and He can keep us operating effectively; He gave us an operator's manual to aid us in life and living.

III. The Value of the Bible through You

A. The best translation. When asked "What is the best translation of the Bible?" E. Schuyler English replies, "The best translation of the Scriptures is the man or woman who lives a godly life in accord with God's Word." Have you heard it said that "You are the only Bible somebody might read"? Thinking of your Christian experience in those terms shows how very important we Christians are to the world. We cannot expect the unsaved person to read the Bible; he has no motivation to do so, nor purpose for it. And, if he does so in order to broaden his knowledge, improve his literary skills, or whatever, he does not come to his reading with the infilling of the Holy Spirit to give him understanding.

These things being true, it is critically important for the believer to see the importance of the Bible—not only *to* and *for* him, but *through* him. Richard W. DeHaan put it this way:

> In his study of the Authorized Version of the Bible someone gathered the following facts: The Scriptures contain 3,586,489 letters, 773,692 words, 31,173 verses, and 1,189 chapters. The word "and" occurs 1,855 times, but the word "reverend" only once. Ezra 7:21 contains all the letters of the alphabet except "J." The longest verse is Esther 8:9, and the shortest in the English language is John 11:35.
>
> So what? Although it's wonderful to have such a deep interest in God's Word that we're willing to spend countless hours compiling this data, what good is gained if these FACTS are not translated into ACTS? . . . . Such a practice reminds me of Paul's word to his son in the faith, Timothy. He refers to the fact that some who are "ever learning . . . never . . . come to the knowledge of the truth" (II Tim. 3:7).

B. Adorning Scripture. It's not simply what we know, but what we act upon. As James puts it, we are to be doers of the Word, not hearers only (James 1:22). The Word, furthermore, must not only work *in* our lives, but *through* our lives. It's almost impossible to overstate the importance of doctrine, the teaching of Scripture. But Paul suggests to Titus that the Christian can add to doctrine in the sense that he makes it attractive, " . . . that they may adorn the doctrine of God our Saviour in all things" (Titus 2:10). As a frame enhances a picture without changing its content in the least, so the life of a believer enhances the truth of God's Word. The frame does not bring attention to itself, it focuses attention upon the picture. The Christian must have the attitude of John the Baptist, "He must increase, but I must decrease" (John 3:30).

Yet, the frame is important. Unless our lives influence the lives of others, bringing them to Christ, pointing them to the Saviour, we are not demonstrating the true value of the Word.

To sum it up, in relation to the Bible, the believer should love it, know it, obey it, and share it. In the words of the psalmist, "How sweet are thy words unto my taste! yea, sweeter than honey to my mouth!" (Psalm 119:103).

Study the Bible to be wise;

Believe it to be safe;

Practice it to be holy.

(Answers to quizzes)

1. Nebuchadnezzar
2. Leah
3. Aaron
4. Abraham
5. Joseph
6. Elisha
7. Moses
8. Gideon
9. Peter
10. Silas
11. Solomon
12. Samson
13. Jonathan
14. Nehemiah
15. Samuel
16. John
17. Stephen
18. Joshua
19. Herod
20. Amos
21. Bethany
22. Carmel
23. Cana
24. Sinai
25. Ai
26. Samaria
27. Ethiopia
28. Egypt
29. Armageddon
30. Patmos
31. Basket
32. Rod
33. Pottage
34. Great fish
35. Manna

Scripture locations

1. Exodus 20
2. Luke 15
3. I Corinthians 15
4. I Thessalonians 4
5. Matthew 13
6. Genesis 3
7. Matthew 14, Mark 6, Luke 9, John 6
8. Matthew 5–7
9. Isaiah 53
10. Daniel 9

ADDITIONAL STUDY GUIDES IN THIS SERIES . . .

GENESIS, John P. Burke, paper, $3.95.

DEUTERONOMY, Bernard N. Schneider, paper, $2.95.

JOSHUA, JUDGES & RUTH, John J. Davis, paper, $2.95.

I & II SAMUEL & I KINGS 1-11, John J. Davis, cloth, $4.95; paper, $3.95.

KINGS & CHRONICLES, John C. Whitcomb, paper, $3.95.

PROVERBS, Charles W. Turner, paper, $2.95.

GOSPEL OF JOHN, Homer A. Kent, Jr., cloth, $4.95; paper, $3.95.

ACTS, Homer A. Kent, Jr., paper, $3.95.

ROMANS, Herman A. Hoyt, paper, $2.95.

I CORINTHIANS, James L. Boyer, cloth, $3.95; paper, $2.95.

GALATIANS, Homer A. Kent, Jr., paper, $2.95.

EPHESIANS, Tom Julien, paper, $2.95.

PHILIPPIANS, David L. Hocking, paper, $2.95.

I & II TIMOTHY, Dean Fetterhoff, paper, $2.95.

HEBREWS, Herman A. Hoyt, paper, $2.95.

JAMES, Roy R. Roberts, paper, $3.50.

I, II, III JOHN, Raymond E. Gingrich, paper, $2.95.

REVELATION, Herman A. Hoyt, paper, $2.95.

THE WORLD OF UNSEEN SPIRITS, Bernard N. Schneider, paper, $2.95.

THE HOLY SPIRIT AND YOU, Bernard N. Schneider, paper, $3.95.

PROPHECY, THINGS TO COME, James L. Boyer, paper, $2.95.

PULPIT WORDS TRANSLATED FOR PEW PEOPLE, Charles W. Turner, paper, $2.95.

Order from your local Christian bookstore or BMH Books, P. O. Box 544, Winona Lake, IN 46590. (Include a check with your order and BMH Books pays all postage charges.)